PizzaPedia

Dedication

To Danielle and Cecily, my pizza monsters and quality assurance team.

ISBN 978-1-4971-0502-7

Library of Congress Control Number: 2024952348

To learn more about the other great books from Fox Chapel Publishing, or to find a retailer near you, call toll-free 800-457-9112 or visit us at www.FoxChapelPublishing.com.

You can also send mail to:
903 Square Street
Mount Joy, PA 17552

We are always looking for talented authors. To submit an idea, please send a brief inquiry to acquisitions@foxchapelpublishing.com.

Printed in China
First printing

PizzaPedia

Favorite Recipes from Across America

Jim Mumford

FOX CHAPEL
PUBLISHING

THIN 174

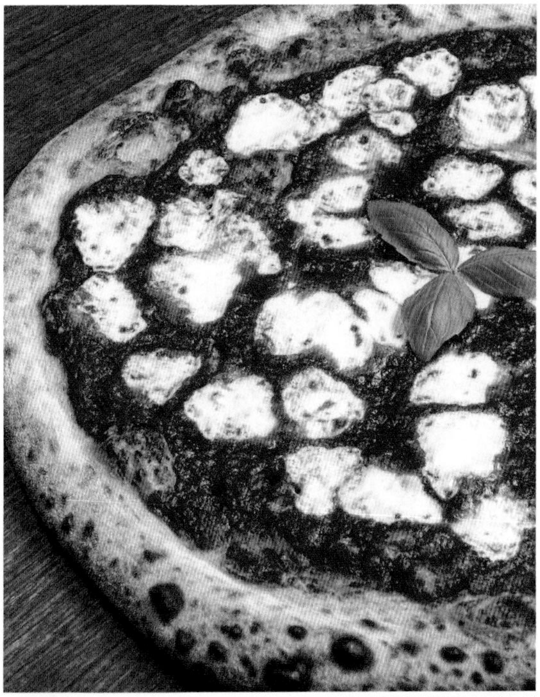

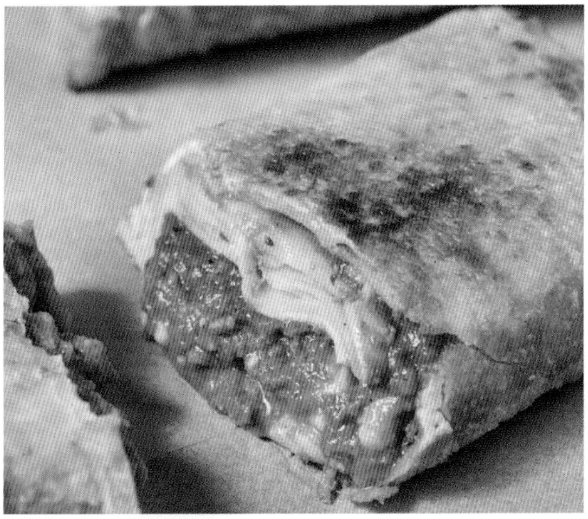

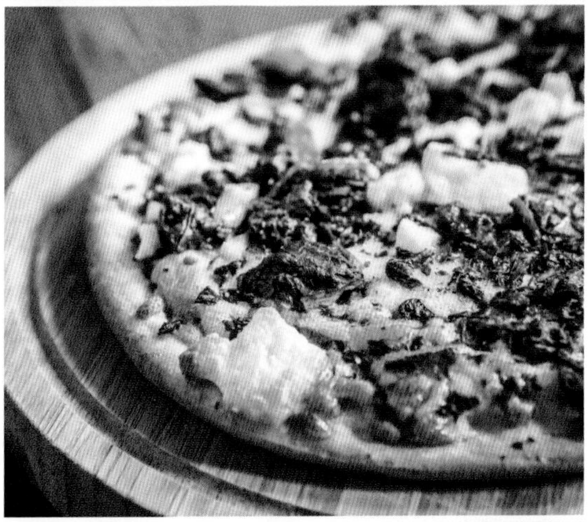

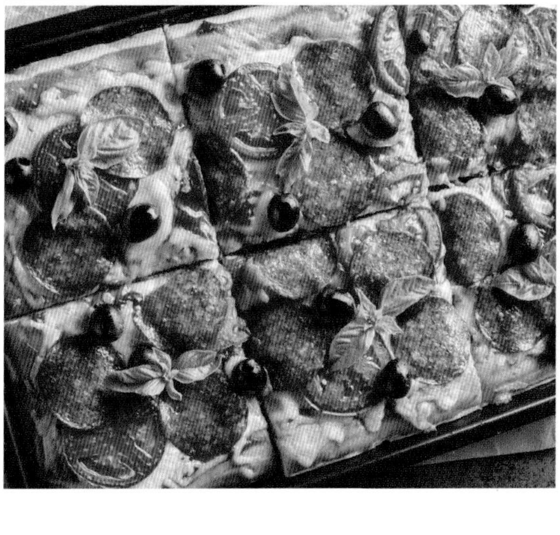

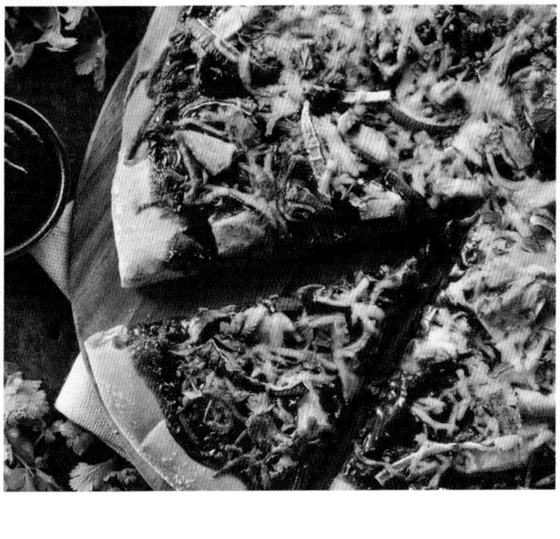

With this book, you can craft your favorite regional pizzas without ever leaving the house.

Introduction

Welcome to *PizzaPedia*, my fellow *pizzaiola* or *pizzaiolo* (which means, you guessed it, "pizza maker"). This book is about to walk you through four main categories of pizza: Neapolitan, pan, Sicilian, and thin crust. More specifically, we are about to embark on a journey across over thirty regional styles of pizza within these four types, highlighting the wonderful nuances that make every region's pie unique and amazing. Within these regional styles are more than 100 variants: from authentic topping combos and traditional bites to adventurous dough swaps and everything in between.

Developing this book was a labor of delicious love. I visited dozens of pizzerias, took many road trips, and consumed more slices of pizza than you can imagine. The result is a "Regional Pizza 101," so to speak, introducing you to each general style and its nuances via recipes inspired by the regional classics and optimized for the home cook. I've also included photos and details from some of my favorite regional pizza spots, so you can visit and compare their professional pies with your own homemade offerings. I hope you find, as I did, that just a few humble pizza ingredients can be combined in so many unique and incredible ways—over 100 of them, to be specific.

Transform simple dough, sauce, and cheese into over 100 unique recipes.

The Right Equipment

No matter the regional style you're paying homage to, the equipment and tools you use play a crucial role. From pizza stones and peels to ovens and cutters, each item you use helps bring out the best of your chosen style. In this section, I'll guide you through must-have tools for achieving authentic, high-quality results.

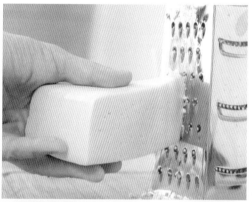

Box Grater—You'll use a box grater to shred and grate some cheeses, depending on the texture you want to achieve. When selecting a box grater, look for sturdy construction with sharp, stainless steel blades. Consider a grater with multiple grating sizes (for example, coarse, medium, and fine) to accommodate both hard and soft cheeses. Choose a model with a large capacity for versatility with other ingredients and make sure it's dishwasher-safe and has a nonslip base or handle.

Microplane—When choosing a microplane for grating hard cheeses, look for a stainless steel blade with sharp, finely spaced teeth. A comfortable, ergonomic handle is essential for easy use, especially when grating larger quantities. Nonslip grips add stability and a light weight enhances maneuverability. You can buy models with catch containers to collect grated cheese. Pick a dishwasher-safe model for easy cleaning.

Digital Scale—When choosing a digital scale for pizza making, look for precision (to at least 0.1 grams), a large weight capacity, and a clear, easy-to-read display. Features like a tare function for subtracting container weight and the ability to display multiple measurement units are also beneficial. A durable design and a flat surface are great options to make your scale easier to clean and to measure with a workbowl on top.

Measure It, Please

The engineer and baking purist in me wanted to list every dough ingredient in grams to ensure the pinnacle of preciseness. Perfection is in the details, and even a tablespoon or two of extra water or flour can cause issues with your dough. That being said, however, this book is meant to make pizza making accessible and enjoyable, not to make you do math—so, you'll notice that all dough ingredients are included in *both* Imperial and metric measurements. All the other ingredients (which don't require the same precision) are listed in Imperial only. **Note:** The recipes here all assume that bread flour at 135g equals 1 cup plus 4½ ounces—your specific brand **will** vary, so it's best to go by weight (grams). Choose the measurement method that gets you in the kitchen, but know that, in my experience, using a scale is far more accurate and makes better pizza every time.

Stand Mixer with Dough Hook Attachment— When selecting a stand mixer for making pizza dough, prioritize models with a powerful motor that can handle thick, heavy mixtures. Look for a sturdy bowl and a range of speed settings for versatility. The hook attachment is essential—it mimics hand kneading, efficiently developing the gluten for a perfect texture. Ensure that the hook is designed to reach all the corners of the bowl for thorough mixing (helical/spiral models work best). Additionally, consider the mixer's capacity to accommodate the amount of dough you will typically prepare. It's hard to have too big of a mixing bowl!

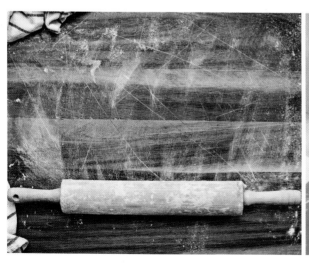

Rolling Pins—Wooden rolling pins offer a traditional feel and excellent grip, providing a good weight that allows for even pressure. Silicone rolling pins are nonstick and easy to clean, reducing the need for flour during rolling. They're lighter and tend to resist sticking and work best on high-moisture doughs. Handled rolling pins tend to work best for pizza, since they provide added control.

Parchment Paper—Parchment paper is a heat-resistant, nonstick paper used in baking and cooking. It helps prevent food from sticking to baking sheets or pans, making for easier cleanup. It can withstand temperatures up to around 450°F (232°C) and is often coated with silicone for additional nonstick capabilities.

Pizza Stone—When selecting a pizza stone, look for materials like ceramic, cordierite, or clay, which retain and distribute heat evenly. Choose a stone that is at least ½" thick for better heat retention and durability. A larger surface area accommodates various pizza sizes, which is always a plus.

A Note on the Pizza Stone

To stone or not to stone? Pizza stones made of tile or other earthenware mimic the deck of a massive pizza oven. Despite their wonderful cooking properties . . . I loathe pizza stones. They are fussy. They take a long time to heat up. And I've broken more than one just by opening the oven and letting in a rush of cold air that cracks the stone. So, how can we get pizza stone benefits without all the fuss? Science.

A pizza stone needs three characteristics: light color, dense yet porous material, and thermal conductivity ("k" value) of 3 W/m-C. (The k value is a measure of how much the stone gives off and takes in heat, measured in watts [W/] per meter [m] per degree Celsius [-C].) All three characteristics allow pizza stones to slowly gain and give off heat, prevent burning, and let moisture escape the dough to create a crisp crust.

Cast iron is dark in color, dense, and has a thermal conductivity of 20–45 W/m-C. It gives up heat much quicker than a pizza stone. Cooking on cast iron alone can be useful for some styles like a pan pizza, but at very high temperatures or for high-hydration doughs it can tend to burn the bottom edges before all of the moisture has a chance to escape in the middle.

Stainless steel is reflective in color, dense, and has a conductivity of 15 W/m-C. It is not very porous, so it isn't great at removing moisture from a pizza like a stone, but it is comparable when it comes to slowly dosing out heat. Stainless steel also heats up quickly and is more forgiving than cast iron, especially at high heats where the window between perfection and over-charred is short.

So, if we want to avoid using a stone, there are options. For smaller pizzas, like the Neapolitan, start the pizza on an inverted cast-iron skillet for a few moments to set the crust, then finish on the rack or a pizza screen to let the dough's moisture properly escape. Alternatively, use a stainless-steel stone for the entire bake, especially for any quick-cooking pies.

Pizza Steel—Look for high-quality materials such as stainless steel or carbon steel when buying a pizza steel, as both provide excellent heat retention and conductivity. A thickness of at least ¼" is ideal for durability and performance. Choose a size that fits your oven while accommodating different pizza sizes. Also consider a steel with a preseasoned surface for easy maintenance and greater nonstick properties. A smooth finish will also simplify cleaning, ensuring longevity and consistent results.

Pizza Peel—When choosing a pizza peel, consider the differences between wooden and metal options. Wooden peels are generally better for launching pizzas, as they allow for easy sliding off the surface and can be less prone to sticking. They also provide a traditional aesthetic. However, they may absorb moisture over time and require more maintenance. Metal peels, on the other hand, are thinner and more rigid, making them ideal for retrieving pizzas from the oven. They heat up quickly, promoting a crispy crust but can be prone to sticking if not adequately floured.

Baking Sheets—When choosing baking sheets, consider materials like aluminum or another dense metal, which heat evenly and resist warping. Or choose nonstick options that promote easy release. Insulated baking sheets provide even heat distribution for delicate items, while darker sheets can promote browning. Look for rimmed edges to better form the crust against. A heavy-duty design is ideal for longevity and consistent performance.

Pizza Pan—Stainless steel pizza pans are durable and resistant to rust, making them a great long-term investment for baking. They heat evenly, ensuring consistent cooking and browning of the crust. Unlike nonstick pans, stainless steel pans require proper oiling or seasoning to prevent sticking, so check the recipe accordingly.

Pizza Crisper—A pizza crisper is a specialized pan designed with perforations to enhance airflow and promote even cooking, resulting in a crispier crust. The holes allow steam to escape, preventing sogginess, making it ideal for thin-crust or pan pizzas. Pizza crispers aren't specifically called for in any of the recipes in this book; however if you find that your crust is less crisp than desired, a 2 to 3 minute finish on a crisper may be in order.

Cast-Iron Pan—Using a cast-iron pan for pizza making offers excellent heat retention and even cooking, resulting in a perfectly crispy crust. Look for a pan that's well seasoned to prevent sticking and enhance flavor. The thickness of the pan contributes to the heat distribution, so choose one that's at least ¼" thick.

Detroit Pan—A Detroit-style pizza pan is typically made of heavy-duty metal, such as aluminum or carbon steel, which promotes even heat distribution for a perfectly baked crust. The pan is usually rectangular with high sides to accommodate the thick crust of Detroit-style pizza. Look for options with nonstick coatings or seasoning to facilitate easy release and cleaning. A sturdy construction is essential to withstand high oven temperatures while ensuring durability for long-term use.

Sicilan Pan—A Sicilian pizza pan is typically square and constructed from durable materials like aluminum or carbon steel, which helps achieve an even bake for the thick crust. Like the Detroit pans, these pans feature high edges to accommodate the Sicilian crust. For easier release and cleaning, look for options with a nonstick surface or those that come preseasoned.

Dutch Oven—A Dutch oven is an excellent choice for frying pizza, as its heavy cast-iron construction provides even heat distribution and retention. Look for a size that fits your pizza (12" is ideal for the recipes in this book). Additionally, consider models with enameled surfaces for easier cleaning and maintenance.

Oven Thermometer—An oven thermometer is an essential tool that ensures your oven is heating to the correct temperature. This device helps achieve precise pizza-making results by allowing you to monitor the temperature inside the oven accurately. For optimal performance, place the thermometer in the center of the oven and check it periodically while preheating.

Additional Thermometers—An *analog thermometer* that clips to the side of the pot (right) is the best option for accurately and safely checking the temperature of oil for frying. An *instant-read digital thermometer* (left) is best for checking the temperature of water or meats. Pick a thermometer that has a quick display time, 0.1 degree accuracy, and a long probe to keep your hands away from hot foods.

Pizza Oven—When selecting an at-home pizza oven, consider the fuel types available, such as wood, charcoal, gas, or pellet. Each fuel type affects the cooking temperature and flavor. Wood provides a traditional smoky taste, while gas offers convenience and ease of use. Pizza ovens often include pizza stones built in or have cooking surfaces that operate in a similar way. Look for ovens with good insulation for heat retention, a cooking surface that can accommodate your pizza size, and a built-in thermometer for accurate temperature readings. Portability and ease of assembly are also key factors to consider if you plan to use your oven outdoors.

Charcoal Grill—A charcoal grill ideal for pizza will provide enough space to accommodate a pizza stone or steel and should be capable of maintaining high temperatures. The ability to control airflow is crucial for managing heat levels, and using a two-zone setup (direct and indirect heat) enhances cooking flexibility. Consider models with adjustable vents and a sturdy construction for durability. A removable ash catcher simplifies cleanup, making it easier to maintain for outdoor cooking sessions.

Gas Grill—A gas grill ideal for cooking pizza will have ample space to fit a pizza stone or steel, and should reach temperatures of at least 700°F (370°C) for optimal cooking. Multiple burners are advantageous for controlling the temperature and employing both direct and indirect cooking methods. Features like a built-in thermometer, adjustable flame control, and durable construction ensure even heat distribution. Portability and ease of cleaning are also important considerations for outdoor use.

Cooling Rack—When choosing a cooling rack for pizza, look for a sturdy design made of stainless steel for durability and heat resistance (you want to make sure the rack won't warp when exposed to heat). A rack with a grid pattern allows for optimal airflow around the pizza, helping to maintain its crispiness as it cools. Ensure that it's large enough to fit your pizza and consider buying a rack that is dishwasher-safe for easy cleaning. Nonslip feet can enhance stability, preventing the rack from sliding off counters during use.

Mezzaluna—When choosing a mezzaluna, stainless steel is the best material. It's durable and rust-resistant. Look for a sharp, curved blade for efficient chopping and a comfortable handle for good grip. There are various types, including single-blade and double-blade designs. Double-blade options offer faster chopping, but for pizza, single-blade is preferred.

Pizza Cutter—When choosing a pizza cutter, look for a sharp, stainless steel blade that will make clean cuts and hold up to regular use. While compact wheel cutters are nice, I prefer the control and speed of a handled model. Consider comfort and grip if choosing a handle—ergonomic designs reduce slipping and accidental pizza damage. A large wheel diameter helps slice through thick crusts effortlessly. Additionally, make sure you opt for something that is dishwasher-safe for easy cleaning.

Ingredients for Success

The ingredients of pizza are simple—dough, cheese, tomatoes, and sometimes toppings—but perfection is in the details. What makes each variant special are the small changes—the order in which you mix the dough ingredients, where you position the pan in the oven, how long you cook the tomatoes, etc. Making each pizza your own is a must, and it's those little differences in ingredients and technique that differentiate a New Haven from a neo-Neapolitan, a Sicilian from a grandma, and so on.

Bottled or Filtered Water—Your tap water is likely terrible for making pizza. Water plays a crucial role in pizza dough, affecting texture, yeast fermentation, and gluten development. Mineral content is key, as elements like chlorine and iron can hinder dough rise and texture. The use of bottled or filtered water ensures consistent rises and textures. Unless you have *fantastic* tap water, use bottled or filtered water (not boiled, which doesn't remove the minerals) for every recipe. It's a minor step, but it's probably the biggest thing you can do to help your pizza come together.

Bread Flour—Bread flour, with a protein content of around 12 percent, provides a versatile dough that balances chew and crispiness. It's ideal for a range of pizza styles, offering structure without being too dense.

00 Flour—00 flour, milled to an ultra-fine texture, is the gold standard for traditional Neapolitan pizza. Its lower protein content, around 11–12 percent, creates a soft, elastic dough that bakes into a tender, airy crust with just the right chew. The fine milling allows for a smooth, easy-to-handle dough, ideal for achieving that authentic thin, blistered pizza base.

Yeast—Dried yeast is available in two types—active dry and instant. Active dry yeast requires reanimation in warm water, while instant yeast can be mixed directly into the dough for quicker results. Opt for yeast sold in airtight jars (typically containing 4 ounces) rather than single packets for better long-term use. Store your yeast in the fridge or freezer after opening to maintain the freshness, ensuring that it stays potent for months.

The Trouble with Yeast

Dried yeast is weird. In short, the little grains are balls of dead yeast cells encapsulating live, dormant yeast. Because yeast is alive, it is a fussier product than one would think. It is not uncommon for the yeast in your grocery store to be old and nearly dead. So, unless you're best friends with a brewer (and if so, consider me jealous), it can be tricky to find good yeast. Look for the freshest you can get and keep it away from heat and light when you do. To help with this, many of my recipes use a "bloom" step to wake up the yeast before proceeding. In any case, if after a few hours you don't notice much going on, you may want to try again.

Crushed Tomatoes—Tomatoes bring sweetness and fruitiness to the pizza. Opt for high-quality crushed tomatoes, like San Marzano, known for their balanced sweetness and low acidity. These Italian tomatoes deliver a deep, authentic flavor that transforms your sauce into something truly special.

Passata—Passata offers a smooth, uncooked, velvety tomato base perfect for pizza. Made from pureed, strained tomatoes, it provides a clean, fresh flavor—look for Italian varieties for the best quality.

Grated Cheese—A key element of pizza is, of course, the cheese. Always grate your own, as pre-grated may have other starches added to help with maintaining texture, which will alter the melt and final quality of the pizza.

Sliced Cheese—More than just for sandwiches, sliced cheese brings a uniform and slower melt and coverage to the pizza. Deli sliced is best, with a "thin" thickness being the best bet for most pies.

Grate Your Own

Pre-shredded cheese is awesomely convenient. Those individual threads of cheese look amazing on a pizza. There's just one problem—those shreds are often treated cornstarch or cellulose (wood pulp/sawdust) so they don't stick together in the bag. That coating messes with the melting of the cheese and leads to some funky results at some of the high temperatures we will be using. So, unless you like goopy cheese on your pizza, grate your own cheese.

A Note on Cheese Varieties

You will see both Parmigiano Reggiano and Parmesan cheeses listed. If the recipe calls for "Parmigiano Reggiano" explicitly, I recommend you use that specific cheese in that specific pizza. If, however, "Parmesan" is listed, you may use either Parmigiano Reggiano or a high-quality American Parmesan cheese. The same goes for Pecorino Romano and Romano cheese.

Parmigiano Reggiano—Parmigiano Reggiano is a prized Italian cheese known for its rich, nutty flavor and granular texture. Made from unpasteurized cow's milk and aged for at least 12 months, it undergoes strict production regulations in designated regions of Italy. The cheese is renowned for its complex taste, which deepens with age, making it ideal for use on pizza both pre- and post-bake. Its authenticity is protected by the PDO/DOP (Protected Designation of Origin/Denominazione di Origine Protetta) label, ensuring that only cheese made in specific regions can bear the name. Parmigiano Reggiano is welcome on just about every pizza, but is best reserved for those with fewer ingredients, where the complexity of the cheese can shine.

Parmesan—American Parmesan cheese differs from Parmigiano Reggiano primarily in production methods and aging. While Parmigiano Reggiano is made from raw cow's milk and aged for a minimum of 12 months under strict regulations in Italy, American Parmesan often uses pasteurized milk and may be aged for shorter periods, resulting in a milder flavor. This difference in ingredients and aging affects the texture and taste, making authentic Parmigiano Reggiano richer and more complex. Parmesan is best used on pizzas that have a multitude of other strong flavors, where the subtle notes of the authentic version would be otherwise muted.

Romano—Romano cheese, particularly Pecorino Romano, is a hard, salty Italian cheese made from sheep's milk. It has a sharp, tangy flavor that intensifies with age, making it excellent for grating over pasta and salads. Unlike Parmigiano Reggiano, which is made from cow's milk, Romano has a distinct taste profile that adds a bold character to dishes. It's typically aged for at least five months and adds a sharp contrasting flavor to pizza, especially when used as a finish.

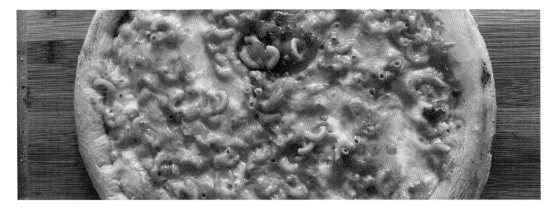

Little things can take an ordinary pizza to new levels—the right techniques can be the difference between a good pizza and an amazing pizza.

Techniques

Your dough is your starting point and provides the structural base for your pizza, so it's important to use the right skills and techniques to transform simple ingredients into a delicious crust. From kneading the dough to rolling and shaping it, the method you use makes all the difference in achieving authentic regional results.

Kneading and Rising

Kneading your dough ingredients develops gluten, creating elasticity and structure. You can knead the dough in a stand mixer or by hand (and dough recipes that require a specific kneading method will tell you in the instructions). The amount of kneading you do and the method used will affect your final results—creating different textures, variations in the cook, and different overall structure.

A helical/spiral kneading hook is the most effective design for pulling in the ingredients from the sides of the bowl.

Hand kneading allows you to have more control over the dough's final consistency.

STAND MIXER KNEADING

Kneading pizza dough in a stand mixer with a dough hook allows for consistent gluten formation, which is essential for achieving the desired texture in the crust. By using specific speeds and mixing times, the dough develops elasticity and strength without overworking it. The dough hook mimics hand kneading, efficiently incorporating air and moisture while keeping the process hands-free, making it easier to achieve a perfectly kneaded dough for that ideal chewiness and rise.

HAND KNEADING

Hand kneading the dough after mixing is essential for achieving a smooth texture and developing gluten strength. While the stand mixer effectively incorporates the ingredients, hand kneading allows for better control over the dough's consistency. This process enhances gluten development, which contributes to elasticity and structure. Additionally, it helps to create a uniform surface, ensuring that the dough rises evenly and results in a well-structured pizza crust.

Forming your dough into a ball prior to the rise does more than perfectly portion it, it also allows for more even fermentation.

"BALLING" THE DOUGH

After rising, we "ball" the dough to create individual portions that allow for even fermentation and shaping. This process helps to strengthen the gluten structure, ensuring a more uniform texture in the final crust. Balling the dough also encourages gas pockets to form, which improves the dough's elasticity and aids in achieving a better rise when baking. The technique sets the stage for a perfectly shaped pizza with a delightful chewiness.

Rolling and Shaping

For many pizza makers, the most daunting part of making pizza is forming or rolling the dough. Fear not, the tips below will help anyone become a true pizza artisan in no time!

BRING THE DOUGH TO ROOM TEMPERATURE

Each style of pizza has different shaping requirements, but one rule that applies to each is that doughs that have been chilled overnight must be brought to room temperature before shaping. This is crucial for easier stretching, ensuring that the dough is pliable. This step also softens the gluten in the dough, making it more workable. While waiting, remove any watches or rings to prevent them from tearing the dough. The recipes provide general advice on when to remove the chilled dough from the fridge.

PREPARE THE WORK SURFACE

Pizza dough can stick to the bench due to its moisture content and gluten development, which makes the dough slightly sticky. Additionally, kneading or shaping without enough flour can increase stickiness. Preparing a workbench with a light dusting of flour creates a clean, nonstick surface for handling the dough. This helps prevent sticking and tearing while shaping or rolling out the dough, ensuring a smoother process. A clean board also minimizes contamination and maintains the integrity of the dough. Proper flouring allows for better control during shaping, resulting in a well-formed pizza crust.

Instead of using a ton of flour (which, if used in excess, can throw off the ratios within the dough), apply a drop or two of olive oil to your hands, as they will be in frequent contact with the dough. Then use a *thin* layer flour on the bench to prevent any further sticking.

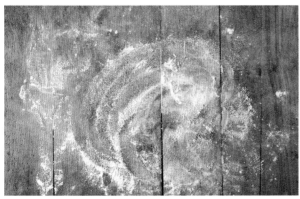

Be careful not to overflour, as the dough may take on too much and dry out—a light dusting is all you need!

If the work surface isn't adequately floured, the dough may stick, making it difficult to handle.

PREPARE YOUR TOOLS

Using a well-floured rolling pin or a clean, silicone rolling pin helps ensure that the dough rolls out evenly without sticking, allowing for easier handling and shaping. Insufficient flour on the pin creates a sticky surface that prevents smooth rolling, while residue on the pin can also cause the dough to adhere.

Transferring the pizza dough from the bench to the pan, stone, or steel once you've finished rolling or shaping is also a very important and tricky part of the process. A pizza peel is the best tool for the job, but an inverted baking sheet or pan can achieve similar results. Preparing the pizza peel (or similar tool) with flour or semolina prevents the dough from sticking, allowing for easy transfer to and from the oven. Flour creates a barrier between the surface and the dough, while semolina also adds extra texture and helps achieve a crispier crust. This preparation ensures that the pizza slides off effortlessly, maintaining its shape and avoiding any tearing. A light coating will do, as an excess will alter cooking time and textures. You can also try covering the surface of your transferring tool with either baking parchment or a sprinkle of cornmeal to prevent sticking.

To transfer dough onto your prepared peel, gently lift the dough from the work surface, using your hands or a bench scraper if needed. Place the dough on the peel and quickly adjust it if necessary to center it. If the dough starts to stick, add a little more flour or semolina to the peel below before moving it to the oven. This method helps maintain the dough's shape and prevents tearing.

Some recipes also have specific requirements for preapring the pan or cooking surface—you may need to oil or grease the pan, add a layer of parchment paper, etc.—it's important to follow these instructions to achieve the right results for your chosen pizza type. To transfer the dough onto your prepared pizza pan, you can use the pizza peel if needed, but you can also use your hands to gently lift the dough from your work surface and place it onto the pan. If needed, you can roll the dough onto a rolling pin, then unroll it onto the pan. Once the dough is on the pan, adjust the shape as necessary, pressing gently to fit the dough into the pan without tearing. This method allows for even cooking and a nicely shaped crust.

Dough will stick to your rolling pin if the pin is underfloured or dirty.

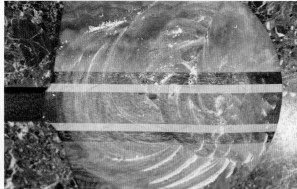

Use just a light coating of flour, semolina, or cornmeal on your pizza peel so the pizza can easily slide off onto the cooking surface.

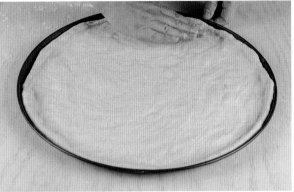

Once your dough is on the peel, adjust it to make sure it's centered.

When pressing your dough into the pan, use gentle pressure to avoid tearing it.

SHAPING NEAPOLITAN PIZZAS

There are a few different methods for shaping Neapolitan pizzas, but the overall process is generally the same for each. After the dough has rested, turn it out onto your prepared bench. Use the palm of your hand to press it into a flattish circle. Gradually spread it out by pressing the center with your fingers, leaving about ½" untouched around the edge for the outer crust.

Continue lightly pressing until the dough is about ½" thick, which should create a uniform circle. If the dough shrinks back only slightly, it's ready and you can continue to the next step. If it snaps back quickly, it needs more resting, so leave it covered with a kitchen towel for 10 to 15 minutes. Repeat the flattening process until you have a well-shaped ½" thick circle.

The fingertip extension technique begins with a flattened disk. You'll work from the center out toward the edges.

Work gently and be sure to leave a ½" of untouched border to ensure you achieve a well-formed crust that rises beautifully in the oven.

FINGERTIP EXTENSION TECHNIQUE

The most basic shaping method is the "fingertip extension technique," which both shapes the dough and helps to maintain its texture. Begin by pressing your fingertips into the flattened disk and gently pushing outward to elongate the dough. Start at the center of the dough, gradually moving toward the outer edge of the crust. Be cautious not to penetrate or overly thin the dough, aiming for a circular shape with a ½" of untouched border around the edge.

Take your time with the knuckle stretch technique and maintain a slow, controlled pace to prevent tears and achieve a beautifully even crust.

This method gives you the advantage of rotating the dough as you stretch, helping you easily spot areas that are uneven in thickness.

KNUCKLE STRETCH

The most popular technique with pizzaiolos, the "knuckle stretch" unsurprisingly involves using your knuckles to stretch the dough. Bring your hands together in a "fist bump" position, placing the flattened dough over your joined hands. Gradually move your fists apart, maintaining a slow and gentle pace to prevent tearing. Simultaneously, circulate the pizza dough so you can observe and quickly identify areas that may be too thin or thick.

The revolving disk technique is effective for achieving a well-formed crust with a consistent thickness throughout, making it a favorite among pizza makers.

The "steering wheel maneuver" lets gravity help you stretch your pizza dough.

REVOLVING DISK METHOD

The "revolving disk method" is very straightforward. Place both hands flat on the dough. As you rotate the dough, pull your hands in opposite directions. The spinning motion ensures a smooth and even foundation, as long as your hands work in opposition during the rotation. By working your hands in opposition, you maintain control over the dough's shape, ensuring that it stretches uniformly.

STEERING WHEEL MANEUVER

Let gravity do some of your work with the "steering wheel maneuver." Grip the edge of the flattened disk, letting the rest of the dough hang straight down. Pinch the edge as you rotate the dough in your hands, allowing it to stretch into a sizable, thin circle. Place the stretched dough above your prepared baking sheet or pizza peel. Check for any uneven areas. Press out thicker parts and thicken thin areas by pinching the dough with your thumb and index finger.

SHAPING PAN, SICILIAN, AND THIN PIZZAS

Most other pizza styles are shaped using a rolling pin. Once you've prepared your work surface and your rolling pin, you'll also want to apply a thin layer of flour to the dough.

To roll out pizza dough, place the lightly floured dough onto the prepared bench. Position the prepared rolling pin in the center of the dough and roll outward in a consistent motion, applying gentle and even pressure. Rotate and flip the dough periodically to maintain the desired shape and continue rolling until the required thickness is achieved. If the dough begins to stick to the rolling pin, add a bit more flour to the surface and the pin to facilitate smoother rolling. This method ensures an even distribution of thickness across the entire pizza crust.

Once the dough is rolled out to the desired size and thickness, carefully transfer it to a prepared pizza peel or cooking surface. As noted earlier, you can drape the rolled-out dough over the rolling pin and then gently unroll it onto the peel or cooking surface. Alternatively, you can fold the dough in half, lift it, and unfold it onto the peel or cooking surface. With the dough in place, gently reshape it into the size and shape specified in the recipe.

When forming dough for pan-style crusts, use your fingertips to create dimples in the surface, which helps the dough rise evenly and creates a light, airy texture.

You'll also want to create dimples with your fingertips for Sicilian-style doughs. Be careful not to overstretch the dough, as you want to maintain its elasticity and texture.

When rolling dough for a thin crust, be sure you evenly roll away from yourself (side-to-side rolling will misshape the dough).

Pizza is incredibly fun and rewarding to craft at home. With these tips, you can avoid many of the common pitfalls home cooks face.

Tips and Tricks

If you're anything like me (and since you're reading this, you probably are), you're eager to get to pizza making. Humor me for a page or two, if you would, and let me share some additional tips to keep in mind as we proceed; I promise each tip will lead to a much better pizza experience!

TRUST YOUR GUT

Repeat after me, "I am a pizza master!" This book is a guide to help you achieve pizza greatness, but *you* are the artisan. If something doesn't look or feel right, trust your pizza master's gut. If the dough seems really dry after the mixing time, add a splash of water. If nothing is rising after hours, try again (it happens to all of us). If it seems like the pizza wants more sauce, sauce away! You're the chef and you know best.

DISTRUST YOUR OVEN

Even the best ovens lie. Or, more accurately, they will cycle within a range of your set temperature. Making matters worse, most ovens are calibrated at a temperature between 350–400°F (177–204°C). At the high heat we will be using, the accuracy may be even worse, causing more variation in temperature (often on the low end).

Oven thermometers are a great idea when baking anything. They're cheap insurance against rogue ovens.

A lot of factors go into the precision and accuracy of your oven, but there are a few things we can do. One, avoid peeking at your pizza every two minutes—if you're looking, you're not cooking. Two, invest in an oven thermometer to make sure the temperature is accurate. Finally, when I say preheat the oven, **preheat** the oven. The longer you can let it preheat, the better off you'll be. Despite all of this, every oven works a little bit differently, and, while I provide cooking ranges, be sure to keep a close eye on your baking until you know how each style works in your oven. Also, should you decide to make multiple pizzas at once, your cooking time may be increased by a few minutes depending on your oven.

TRIBUTES, NOT COPIES

There are 30 pizzerias mentioned in this book, places I adore that provided culinary inspiration for the 100-plus recipes in this book. That being said, none of the recipes written are intended to copy them or are versions of their recipes. Instead, the recipes are tributes inspired by their legendary pies, but crafted for the home cook and the tools and skills at their disposal. I highly encourage you to make these pizzas at home, then visit and try the pizzeria's version. That is the best way to experience the entire range of what that specific pie has to offer!

HAVE FUN!

Even oblong, messy pizza is really good pizza. Have fun with your pizza adventure, and don't you *dare* take this too seriously! Most importantly, share your creations with as many friends and family members as you can.

Additional Resources

If a picture is worth a thousand words, then a video must be worth a million. The three creators listed here are my go-to resources for anything and everything pizza-related. On their pages, you can find even more tips and tricks, as well as how-to guides and videos on rolling, forming, and crafting pizzas of all kinds.

- Christy Alia (*@realcleverfood*) is an award-winning pizza maker, host of pizza- and bread-making classes, the founder of Women's Pizza Month, and an incredible photographer who provided many of the shots in this book. Christy also has many pizza-making tutorials on her Instagram, giving you (and me) all of her expert insights on making the perfect pie.
- Jimmy Henry (*@jimmyhank_pizza*), also known as "The Frico King," is a master of Detroit- and Sicilian-style pies (he invented a spatula just for Detroit-style pies, so you know he is legit). Jimmy also has a wealth of knowledge to share on his Instagram and is a must-follow for any pizza maker.
- The North American Pizza & Culinary Academy (*@pizzaculinaryacademy*), led by Anthony Iannone, is a wonderful resource for pizza tutorials and classes. A pizza maker's pizza maker, Anthony and his team are all world-class, highly knowledgeable individuals on all types of pizza. Their videos walk through making classic pizzas step by step, showing a true artisan's touch.

Neapolitan *Style*

Neapolitan pizza is the embodiment of Italian simplicity and tradition, tracing its roots back to Naples. This style is known for its soft, thin crust with a slightly chewy texture and characteristic charring. Cooked in blistering-hot ovens, Neapolitan pizza achieves a unique lightness while maintaining a flavorful, airy crust. Authentic Neapolitan pizzas focus on just a few high-quality ingredients, like San Marzano tomatoes, fresh mozzarella, and basil, creating a pizza that is as elegant as it is delicious. Regional takes on Neapolitan pizza, particularly in places like New York, New Haven, and California, have adopted this style, often adding creative toppings and adapting the baking techniques to suit modern kitchens while preserving the essence of this Italian classic.

The Neapolitan, one of the oldest styles of pizza, is a classic for a reason; the high heat transforms the simple ingredients into something magical.

Traditional Neapolitan

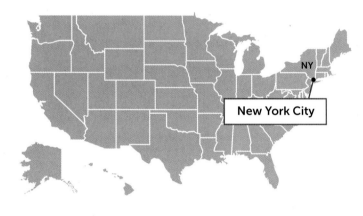

According to the Associazione Verace Pizza Napoletana (AVPN; *https://www.pizzanapoletana.org/en/ricetta_pizza_napoletana*), genuine Neapolitan pizza dough is made with wheat flour, yeast, salt, and water. Simplicity is peak Italian cooking, and this pizza that hails from Naples is just that. Focusing on the quality of the ingredients and the method used is more important than anything with this classic, old-world pie. To that end, there are *very specific* rules on what can be called a Neapolitan pizza, which can be found on the AVPN website. These guidelines call out water content, protein percentages, and water absorption, among other things.

The Napoletana dough recipe here is based on the AVPN guidelines, in case you ever want to formally compete in a sanctioned event. Back-calculated from the metric, this is a recipe that you will want to weigh. Hand kneading your dough is most authentic, but using a stand mixer is perfectly fine by me. **Note:** An authentic cook occurs at about 800–850°F (425–450°C), which is only truly possible in an outdoor pizza oven.

NAPOLETANA DOUGH

MAKES ONE 12" PIZZA

Ingredients
- 1¼ cups (167g) **00 flour**
- ⅓ cup, plus a splash (100mL) **water**
- ⅙ teaspoon (0.5g) **active dry yeast**
- ¾ teaspoon (4.5g) **table salt**

1 In your stand mixer or a large bowl, gently combine the flour, water, yeast, and salt. Knead for 5 minutes on low speed.

2 Let the dough rise on the counter for 4 hours, then form it into a clean ball.

3 Move the dough into the refrigerator overnight.

4 On pizza day, remove the dough from the refrigerator 3 hours before cooking.

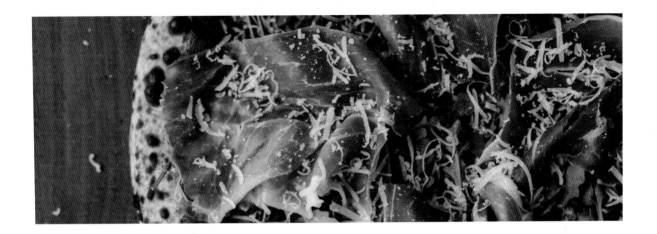

Gluten-Free Alternative

Gluten-free? No problem! The quality of GF flours has come a long, long way in recent years, going from a chalky dough to a product that highly resembles traditional flours and works great both in the home oven and pizza oven alike. I use Caputo Fioreglut Gluten Free Flour, because I find it to be the closest to traditional flour and the easiest to work with. Feel free to use your favorite GF flour, just note that some trial and error will be needed. See page 39 for a full recipe using the gluten-free Neapolitan dough.

GLUTEN-FREE NEAPOLITAN DOUGH

MAKES TWO 12" TO 14" PIZZAS

Ingredients

- 3⅙ cups (285g) **Caputo Fioreglut Gluten Free Flour**
- 1 cup (225g) **water, warmed to 100°F** (38°C)
- 1½ teaspoons (9g) **salt**
- 2 teaspoons (6g) **instant yeast**
- 2 teaspoons (11g) **olive oil**

1 In the work bowl of your stand mixer, combine the water, yeast, and olive oil.

2 Slowly add in the flour and salt and work on low using the hook attachment for 5 to 10 minutes.

3 Cover and let the dough rise for 1 to 2 hours.

4 When the dough has about doubled, divide it in half and let it proof in the refrigerator for another 3 to 4 hours until it doubles again.

Pizza Napoletana
Pizza Marinara

Our first recipe is a *verace* pizza Napoletana pizza marinara, a cheese-less pie that is the ideal starting point for our Neapolitan journey. The addition of capers is optional for a pizza marinara, but the added briny bite brings a lot to this straightforward pizza.

Ingredients

- Napoletana dough, see page 30
- 3 tablespoons passata or tomato puree
- 2 cloves garlic, sliced thin
- ½ teaspoon dried oregano
- 2 tablespoons capers (optional)
- Olive oil for drizzling

Equipment

- Outdoor pizza oven or cast-iron skillet, pizza stone, or pizza steel

1 Remove the prepared dough from the refrigerator 3 hours before cooking.

2 Fire the outdoor oven to 750–800°F (400–425°C) and preheat the pizza stone for 20 to 30 minutes. **Note:** See the sidebar on page 33 if you don't have an outdoor oven available.

3 Form the dough ball into a 12" pizza with a significant lip.

4 Top with the passata, garlic, and oregano.

5 Cook the pizza for 60 to 90 seconds, using a heat-safe peel or spatula to rotate the pizza every 20 seconds.

6 Once cooked, remove the pizza from the oven. Finish with a drizzle of oil, add a sprinkling of capers, and enjoy!

A classic marinara pie with capers is perhaps not fully traditional, but the briny caper bite is incredible against the tomato goodness.

Alternative Cooking Methods

No outdoor oven? No problem! We can still make an excellent Neapolitan pie. Create a 12" pizza as in the recipe and preheat the oven and an inverted cast-iron skillet, pizza stone, or pizza steel to 500°F (260°C) for 15 minutes.

If using cast iron, bake on the inverted cast iron for 2 minutes or until the crust is just set. Then, remove the pizza from the cast iron and finish it directly on the rack of the oven for another 5–6 minutes or until it is charred and wonderfully golden.

If using a pizza stone or pizza steel, bake directly on the stone or steel for 7–8 minutes or until the crust is set and crisp.

Pizza Margherita

The next stage in our Neapolitan journey is the pizza Margherita, a pie most people associate with this style of pizza. We will also begin to deviate from AVPN rules when it comes to sauces and toppings; don't tell the Italians. A Margherita is the timeless trio of tomatoes, mozzarella, and basil that dates back over 100 years. The commonly accepted lore behind its origin is from 1889 when Queen Margherita of Savoy and her husband, King Umberto I, visited Naples. The queen wanted to try Neapolitan pizza, a popular dish among the common people. To honor her visit, a Neapolitan pizzaiolo named Raffaele Esposito created a pizza to symbolize the Italian flag. It had three primary ingredients: tomatoes (red), mozzarella cheese (white), and basil (green). The queen apparently approved, and it was named the "Margherita" in her honor.

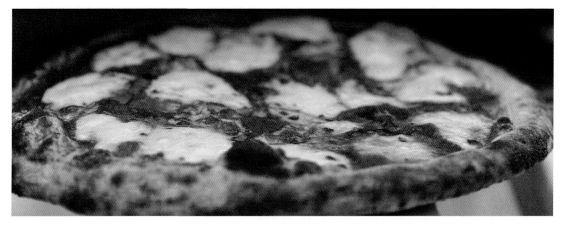

The OG pizza, a Neapolitan Margherita, is simplicity at its finest. The high heat of the oven makes a signature flavor in the crust and caramelizes the tomato in such a perfect way.

Ingredients

- Napoletana dough, see page 30
- ¼ cup passata or tomato puree
- 4 ounces fresh mozzarella, sliced into ½" pieces and drained
- 3 tablespoons extra-virgin olive oil
- 8–10 basil leaves

Equipment

- Outdoor pizza oven or cast-iron skillet, pizza stone, or pizza steel

1 Remove the prepared dough from the refrigerator 3 hours before cooking.

2 Fire the outdoor oven to 750–800°F (400–425°C) and preheat the pizza stone for 20 to 30 minutes. **Note:** See the sidebar on page 33 if you don't have an outdoor oven available.

3 Roll out the dough into a 12" pie.

4 Top with the passata, a pinch of salt, mozzarella, and a drizzle of olive oil.

5 Cook the pizza for 60 to 90 seconds, using a heat-safe peel or spatula to rotate the pizza every 20 seconds.

6 Once cooked, remove the pizza from the oven. Finish with the basil leaves.

Burrata Margherita

A variant of the classic Margherita pie features burrata cheese instead of mozzarella. Burrata cheese is a type of Italian cheese known for its creamy and indulgent texture. It is made from fresh mozzarella, but with a unique twist. The outer layer is solid mozzarella, while the inside contains a mix of mozzarella and cream, resulting in a soft, buttery, and rich filling that oozes when cut open. The resulting pizza is a symphony of not only flavors but textures.

Take a moment to celebrate all that rich burrata, which brings not only a creamy flavor, but adds a smooth, velvety texture to the slice.

Ingredients

- Napoletana dough, see page 30
- ¼ cup passata or tomato puree
- 4 ounces fresh burrata cheese
- 3 tablespoons extra-virgin olive oil
- 8–10 basil leaves

Equipment

- Outdoor pizza oven or cast-iron skillet, pizza stone, or pizza steel

1 Remove the prepared dough from the refrigerator 3 hours before cooking.

2 Fire the outdoor oven to 750–800°F (400–425°C) and preheat the pizza stone for 20 to 30 minutes. **Note:** See the sidebar on page 33 if you don't have an outdoor oven available.

3 Roll out the dough into a 12" pie.

4 Top with the passata, a pinch of salt, and a drizzle of olive oil.

5 Cook the pizza for 60 to 90 seconds, using a heat-safe peel or spatula to rotate the pizza every 20 seconds.

6 Once cooked, remove the pizza from the oven. Finish with pulls of the fresh burrata and the basil leaves, along with another drizzle of olive oil.

Contadina Margherita

There are dozens, if not hundreds, of world-class Neapolitan pizza makers across the country, many in the greater New York area. In my travels, however, I've had the pleasure of meeting a Neapolitan pizzaiola who rivals any and all: Anna Crucitt. Trained as a gelato chef, Anna picked up the pizza trade from her brothers, Michael and Joe Mercurio. A World Pizza Champion and Ambassador for Women in Pizza, Anna runs Mercurio's in Pittsburgh, Pennsylvania, and produces some of the most adventurous and stunning pizzas on the planet. Chef Anna features many pies, from classics to chef-crafted combinations. Her Margherita Contadina truly stands out to me. This creation features eggplant and roasted red peppers against a Margherita backdrop—it's a stunning combination. Our version is based on her masterpiece; while *contadina* may mean "peasant" in Italian, this pizza is fit for royalty.

The combination of the earthy eggplant and the sweet, roasted peppers makes for a complex, ultra savory bite when paired with the lightly charred crust.

Ingredients

- Napoletana dough, see page 30
- ¼ cup passata or tomato puree
- 4 thin slices eggplant, roasted
- 4 ounces fresh mozzarella, sliced into ½" pieces and drained
- ¼ cup roasted red peppers, cut into strips
- 3 tablespoons extra-virgin olive oil
- 8–10 basil leaves

Equipment

- Outdoor pizza oven or cast-iron skillet, pizza stone, or pizza steel

1 Remove the prepared dough from the refrigerator 3 hours before cooking.

2 Fire the outdoor oven to 750–800°F (400–425°C) and preheat the pizza stone for 20 to 30 minutes. **Note:** See the sidebar on page 33 if you don't have an outdoor oven available.

3 Roll out the dough into a 12" pie.

4 Top with the passata, a pinch of salt, roasted eggplant, mozzarella, roasted red peppers, and a drizzle of olive oil.

5 Cook the pizza for 60 to 90 seconds, using a heat-safe peel or spatula to rotate the pizza every 20 seconds.

6 Once cooked, remove the pizza from the oven. Finish with the basil leaves and another drizzle of olive oil.

Inspiration:
The bright and roasted flavors stand out on Chef Anna Crucitt's pizza, making the final product lighter and giving summery vibes with every bite.

Prosciutto Neapolitan

Chef Anna Crucitt's other masterpiece is the Pizza della Casa, or "house pizza." Again, she uses a Margherita base, but now she adds copious amounts of prosciutto to take the pizza to another level. Our version will feature most of the same ingredients—why mess with perfection? When in Rome (or Naples), do as Chef Anna does.

Here, the spicy arugula is low-key the star, cutting through the savory and rich flavors perfectly.

Inspiration: The salty prosciutto adds incredible umami to Chef Anna's pizza, creating a slice that is a cross between classic pizza flavors and an Italian deli sandwich.

Ingredients
- Napoletana dough, see page 30
- ¼ cup passata or tomato puree
- 4 ounces fresh mozzarella, sliced into ½" pieces and drained
- 6 cherry tomatoes, halved
- 3 tablespoons extra-virgin olive oil
- 6 slices prosciutto
- ¼ cup fresh arugula
- 8–10 basil leaves
- 1 ounce Parmigiano Reggiano, shaved

Equipment
- Outdoor pizza oven or cast-iron skillet, pizza stone, or pizza steel

1 Remove the prepared dough from the refrigerator 3 hours before cooking.

2 Fire the outdoor oven to 750–800°F (400–425°C) and preheat the pizza stone for 20 to 30 minutes. **Note:** See the sidebar on page 33 if you don't have an outdoor oven available.

3 Roll out the dough into a 12" pie.

4 Top with the passata, a pinch of salt, mozzarella, cherry tomatoes, prosciutto, and a drizzle of olive oil.

5 Cook the pizza for 60 to 90 seconds, using a heat-safe peel or spatula to rotate the pizza every 20 seconds.

6 Once cooked, remove the pizza from the oven. Finish with the arugula, basil leaves, and Parmigiano Reggiano, along with another drizzle of olive oil.

Gluten-Free Neapolitan

The gluten-free Neapolitan is considered by many to be the most difficult GF pizza to make. Using the right flour and some purposeful technique, however, we can craft a dough that mimics the original pie. Note the high water content, which is necessary when working with GF flour; don't be alarmed if this dough is on the sticky side compared to others you may encounter.

This looks and tastes just like wheat flour pizza—you'd never know this was gluten free.

Ingredients

- Gluten-free Napoletana dough, see page 31
- ¼ cup passata or tomato puree
- 4 ounces fresh mozzarella, sliced into ½" pieces and drained
- 3 tablespoons extra-virgin olive oil
- 8–10 basil leaves

Equipment

- Outdoor pizza oven or cast-iron skillet, pizza stone, or pizza steel

1 Remove the prepared dough from the refrigerator and let it come to room temperature.

2 Fire the outdoor oven to 750–800°F (400–425°C) and preheat the pizza stone for 20 to 30 minutes. **Note:** See the sidebar on page 33 if you don't have an outdoor oven available.

3 Form the dough ball into a 12" pizza with a significant lip.

4 Top with the passata, a pinch of salt, mozzarella, and a drizzle of olive oil.

5 Cook the pizza for 60 to 90 seconds, using a heat-safe peel or spatula to rotate the pizza every 20 seconds.

6 Once cooked, remove the pizza from the oven. Finish with a drizzle of olive oil and the basil leaves.

Manhattan

Of all the ingredients in a pizza, perhaps the water is the most underrated. You see, your tap water has . . . *stuff* . . . in it. Fluoride, minerals, trace amounts of salt, and other by-products of water treatment. While these trace additives may not change the taste, they will affect the way the yeast ferments within the dough as well as the gluten formation during the knead and rise.

Speaking of water, ever wonder why the bagels in New York City *seem* to just taste better? It's partially the same reason pizza in New York is so fantastic—it's in (or, in this case, not in), the water!

I reviewed dozens of municipal water reports from cities around the nation. Most cities have everything discussed above, except for New York! NYC draws its water from rainwater runoff from the Catskill Mountains and treats it minimally, resulting in a more neutral pH and lower amounts of trace minerals. The result in your pizza? A fantastic crisp dough with a more consistent rise, creating a delightfully perfect texture every time. This is especially important in long, cold rises like this one, where the slower fermentation can more easily be halted.

MANHATTAN PIZZA DOUGH

MAKES TWO 10" PIZZAS OR ONE 14" PIZZA

Ingredients

- 2 cups (270g) bread flour
- ¾ cup (175mL) bottled water, warmed to 100°F (38°C)
- 2 teaspoons (8g) sugar
- 1½ teaspoons (4.5g) instant yeast
- 1 tablespoon (14g) olive oil (14g)
- ¾ teaspoon (4.5g) salt

1 In your stand mixer or a large bowl, combine the flour, water, sugar, yeast, oil, and salt. Let mix for 7 minutes on medium-low speed.

2 Once mixed, form the dough into a ball and cover it with plastic wrap. Let it rise for 3–4 hours.

3 Following this proof, let the dough rise in the fridge for 1–2 days, punching it down after the first day.

4 Remove the dough from the refrigerator 2 hours before cooking.

MANHATTAN PIZZA SAUCE

MAKES TWO 10" PIZZAS OR ONE 14" PIZZA

Ingredients

- 2 tablespoons butter
- 2 cloves garlic, minced
- ¾ cup crushed tomatoes
- 1 tablespoon Italian seasoning (mine is equal parts basil, oregano, and parsley)
- ½ teaspoon red pepper flakes

1 Place a saucepot over medium heat and add in the butter.

2 Add the garlic to the pot and stir for 1 minute, then add the crushed tomatoes, Italian seasoning, red pepper flakes, and a pinch of salt.

3 Simmer on low for 15 minutes, then let the sauce cool and set it aside for future use.

Cheese Manhattan Pizza

The classic New York slice, this Manhattan pizza is close to neo-Neapolitan style (see page 47), but a bit fluffier and with more cheese. This is the ideal hand-tossed pizza you have in your mind, the one emulated in pizzerias everywhere. No secrets here, just a straightforward, foldable slice that wins every time. Feel free to double the recipe and make an 18" pizza (provided you have a pizza pan or metal peel big enough).

Folding the pie is optional (but recommended); the slice is traditionally very soft and floppy, hence why so many make a middle fold to facilitate consumption.

Ingredients
- Manhattan pizza dough, see page 40
- Manhattan pizza sauce, see page 40
- 8 ounces mozzarella cheese, grated

Equipment
- 14" pizza pan, pizza steel, or pizza stone

1 Remove the prepared dough from the refrigerator 2 hours before cooking.

2 Prepare the sauce.

3 Preheat the oven to 475°F (245°C), and place the pizza pan, pizza steel, or pizza stone in the oven to preheat.

4 Place the dough ball on a floured surface and stretch it out into a 14" circle.

5 Transfer the dough to the pizza peel or other device you will use to get it into the oven. Top it with the sauce, then the cheese (leaving a ½" lip around the outside edge).

6 Bake for 12–15 minutes or until golden and puffy.

Spinach Pie Manhattan Pizza

A cross between the white pie (page 44) and spinach dip, don't you dare sleep on this pizza. The bitter, earthy tang of the spinach shines in the high heat of the oven, making roasted flavors that bring out the subtle sweetness of the ricotta. Think of this as the ultimate way to sneak in some veggies on pizza night.

Somewhere between classic gameday spinach dip and pizza, this earthy, salty bite is familiar in flavor but certainly surprising on a pie.

Ingredients
- Manhattan pizza dough, see page 40
- 3 tablespoons olive oil
- 6 ounces mozzarella cheese, grated
- ½ cup spinach, cooked and drained
- 3 cloves of garlic, minced
- ½ cup whole milk ricotta cheese

Equipment
- 14" pizza pan, pizza steel, or pizza stone

Try finishing this pie with pulls of burrata instead of the ricotta dollops to create a slightly different flavor and texture.

1 Remove the prepared dough from the refrigerator 2 hours before cooking.

2 Preheat the oven to 475°F (245°C), and place the pizza pan, pizza steel, or pizza stone in the oven to preheat.

3 Place the dough ball on a floured surface and stretch it out into a 14" circle.

4 Transfer the dough to the pizza peel or other device you will use to get it into the oven. Top it with the olive oil, mozzarella, spinach, and garlic.

5 Bake for 12–15 minutes or until golden and puffy. Finish with dollops of ricotta while warm.

Greek Manhattan Pizza

A Greek pizza (by toppings, not by dough) is a fun favorite in many pizzerias, and for good reason. The feta does a lot of the culinary heavy lifting on this one, adding in that tangy, salty layer that ties the onions, olives, and peppers together. It's a harmonious blend that balances savory and zesty notes, creating a truly satisfying experience for pizza lovers.

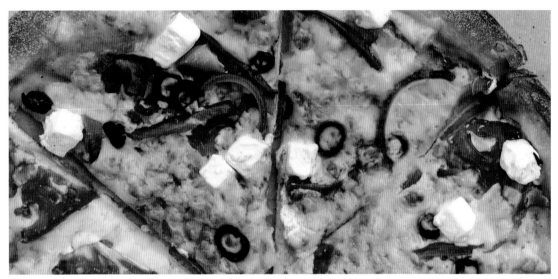

More pizzas should have feta as a finish. The cheese gives a noticeable salty quality that plays with the other flavors perfectly.

Ingredients
- Manhattan pizza dough, see page 40
- Manhattan pizza sauce, see page 40
- 6 ounces mozzarella cheese, grated
- ½ red bell pepper, sliced
- ¼ cup red onion, sliced
- ¼ cup black olives, sliced
- 2 ounces feta cheese, crumbled
- Olive oil for drizzling

Equipment
- 14" pizza pan

1 Remove the prepared dough from the refrigerator 2 hours before cooking.

2 Prepare the sauce.

3 Preheat the oven to 475°F (245°C), and place the pizza pan in the oven to preheat.

4 Place the dough ball on a floured surface and stretch it out into a 14" circle.

5 Transfer the dough to the pizza peel or other device you will use to get it into the oven. Top it with the sauce, mozzarella, red pepper, onion, olives, and feta.

6 Bake for 12–15 minutes or until golden and puffy. Finish with a drizzle of olive oil.

White Manhattan Pizza

There is something magic about a white pie, where the subtle flavors of the cheese play with the bold punches from the garlic and basil. It's a nice changeup that, if cut into strips, also makes a very fun play on cheesy garlic bread. The provolone brings a bit of a switch to the mozzarella, as well—a trick borrowed from many a New York pizzeria.

Ingredients

- Manhattan pizza dough, see page 40
- 3 tablespoons olive oil, plus more for drizzling
- 4 ounces mozzarella cheese, grated
- 2 ounces provolone cheese, grated
- 2 ounces burrata cheese
- 3 cloves of garlic, minced
- 8–10 fresh basil leaves

Equipment

- 14" pizza pan, pizza steel, or pizza stone

1 Remove the prepared dough from the refrigerator 2 hours before cooking.

2 Preheat the oven to 475°F (245°C), and place the pizza pan, pizza steel, or pizza stone in the oven to preheat.

3 Place the dough ball on a floured surface and stretch it out into a 14" circle.

4 Transfer the dough to the pizza peel or other device you will use to get it into the oven. Top it with the olive oil, mozzarella and provolone cheeses, pulls of burrata, and garlic.

5 Bake for 12–15 minutes or until golden and puffy. Finish with the basil leaves and another drizzle of olive oil.

The three-cheese blend, paired with the fierce garlic, makes a deliciously gooey, familiar bite somewhere between garlic bread and alfredo sauce.

Mac and Cheese Pizza

As with the other New York variants, there are many, many wonderful spots to choose from in NYC. To avoid playing favorite to my friends out east, I'm going to highlight one from Chicago instead. Dimo's Pizza holds a special place in my heart, likely due to my post–baseball game tradition of grabbing a slice (or three!). And, though they are 1,000 miles from Manhattan, their pizza is a wonderful representation of what this style is all about. Soft, yet crispy and not shying away from bold toppings, this is the pizza that you think of when you think of a New York slice.

Dimo's is known for their far-out toppings, but for me, there is one must-have every time I visit: the Mac and Cheese Pizza. This pizza is a wonderful exploration of textures. Serve with hot sauce and extra napkins.

Cheesy, crunchy, and chewy, this is a perfect bite. Finish with an acidic hot sauce to bring out the best of the bready and savory flavors in the slice.

Inspiration: While at first glance this is just loading carbs, when contrasted against the creamy cheese and crunchy crust, the elbows on Dimo's creation bring a bite that is unrivaled.

Ingredients
- Manhattan pizza dough, see page 40
- ⅔ cup elbow macaroni, cooked
- 5 ounces cheddar cheese, grated
- 3 ounces mozzarella cheese, grated

Equipment
- 14" pizza pan

1 Remove the prepared dough from the refrigerator 2 hours before cooking.

2 Preheat the oven to 475°F (245°C), and place the pizza pan in the oven to preheat.

3 Place the dough ball on a floured surface and stretch it out into a 14" circle.

4 Transfer the dough to the pizza peel or other device you will use to get it into the oven. Top it with half the pasta, then all the cheddar and mozzarella, and finally the remaining pasta.

5 Lower the oven temperature to 425°F (220°C) and bake for 13–16 minutes, checking often.

Neo-Neapolitan

NY

New York City

This style or variant of the Neapolitan pizza is referred to as neo-Neapolitan, or contemporary Neapolitan. In short, this is the modern version of the classic Neapolitan pie, where the "rules" (like hydration, cooking method, etc.) aren't as strictly enforced. A neo-Neapolitan may also have a little more crunch and texture than the classic Neapolitan.

NEO-NEAPOLITAN DOUGH

MAKES ONE 12" PIZZA

Ingredients

- 1½ cups (200g) **bread flour**
- ½ cup (125mL) **bottled water, plus a splash, warmed to 100°F** (38°C)
- 1 tablespoon (14g) **olive oil, plus more for topping**
- 1 teaspoon (3g) **active dry yeast**
- 1½ teaspoons (6g) **sugar**
- ¾ teaspoon (4g) **table salt**

1 In your stand mixer or a large bowl, combine the water, oil, yeast, sugar, and 1 cup of flour. Work until just combined, about 2 minutes. Let stand for 3 minutes.

2 Following the rest period, begin to mix on low, using the hook attachment on your stand mixer. Gently pour in the remaining flour and the salt. Let mix for 5 minutes on medium-low speed.

3 Once mixed, form the dough into a ball and cover it with plastic wrap. Let the dough proof on the counter for 3–4 hours.

4 After the proof, punch down the dough, refold it into a ball, and let it rise in the fridge for 1–2 days.

5 On pizza day, remove the dough from the refrigerator 2 hours before cooking.

Neo-Neapolitan Cheese

We start with a classic cheese pie, though with perhaps a bit of a twist. By using cubed cheese, we get more of a contrast, since the sauce sees more direct heat and caramelizes more than on a standard pie—a little wrinkle that fits in well with this modern style. Overall, this features more complexity in flavors and textures than you'd expect, but that is the beauty of a neo-Neapolitan pizza!

Inspiration: Jim Henry (see page 27), is a master of Detroit- and Sicilian-style pizza, but he excels at neo-Neapolitan, too. The cubed cheese on his pie makes for a really unique texture and is worth the extra effort.

Ingredients
- Neo-Neopolitan dough, see page 47
- ½ cup passata or tomato puree
- 6 ounces mozzarella cheese, cut into ¾" cubes
- 3 basil leaves
- Olive oil, for brushing

Equipment
- Pizza stone or pizza steel
- Pizza peel

1 Remove the prepared dough from the refrigerator 2 hours before cooking.

2 Preheat the oven to 500°F (260°C) and place your pizza stone or pizza steel in the middle of the oven.

3 Place the dough ball on a floured surface and roll it out into a 12"–14" circle.

4 Transfer the dough to your favorite pizza peel, then top with the passata, a pinch of salt, and the cheese cubes (leaving a ½" lip around the edge). Lightly brush the outer crust with olive oil.

5 Slide the pizza onto the pizza stone or pizza steel and bake it for 9–13 minutes or until golden and puffy. Garnish with the basil, cut, and enjoy!

New York Pepperoni

I'm not saying there's a secret to this one, but if I was going to, it would certainly be the hand-cut pepperoni. The thicker slices add a texture that is wonderful against the crispy and chewy pizza. Also note the herbal additions to the sauce, which better highlight the spicy pepperoni. Finally, we spike this pie with both provolone and Pecorino Romano, adding some buttery and tangy notes. This one is a classic, and for very good reason.

The pepperoni is just perfect for this style—notice how the edges are crisp, but the interior has just set, showcasing the range of what this simple sausage can become.

Ingredients

- Neo-Neopolitan dough, see page 47
- ½ cup passata
- ½ teaspoon dried parsley
- ½ teaspoon dried basil
- ½ teaspoon dried oregano
- ½ teaspoon salt
- 4 ounces mozzarella cheese, grated
- 2 ounces provolone cheese, grated
- 1 ounce Pecorino Romano cheese, grated
- 3 ounces pepperoni, hand sliced

Equipment

- Pizza stone or pizza steel
- Pizza peel

1 Remove the prepared dough from the refrigerator 2 hours before cooking.

2 Preheat the oven to 500°F (260°C) and place your pizza stone or pizza steel in the middle of the oven.

3 Place the dough ball on a floured surface and roll it out into a 12"–14" circle.

4 Prepare the sauce by combining the passata, dried herbs, and salt.

5 Transfer the dough to your favorite pizza peel, then top with the sauce, mozzarella, provolone, Pecorino Romano, and hand-cut pepperoni.

6 Slide the pizza onto the pizza stone or pizza steel and bake it for 10–14 minutes or until just charred and puffy.

Brooklyn Margherita

When I think of a true pizza artisan, Auggie Russo comes to mind. Auggie, who runs Tiny Pizza Kitchen in Brooklyn, is a true master who has perfected the new wave of the neo-Neapolitan pie. The impressive part about Auggie, aside from the fact that he prioritizes the use of farm-fresh ingredients, is how his sheer creativity shows in every pie. The true test of a pizzaiolo is how well they nail their Margherita, and Auggie gets an 11 / 10 for his. Our version is in homage to his, which stars a charred crust against a backdrop of sweet sauce and tangy cheeses.

The char bubbles on the crust are the best part, capturing a bit of the roasted goodness from the oven.

Ingredients

- Neo-Neapolitan dough, see page 47
- ½ cup passata
- 3 ounces fresh mozzarella cheese, sliced into ½" thick rounds and patted dry
- 2 tablespoons Romano cheese
- 2 tablespoons olive oil
- 10 basil leaves

Equipment

- Pizza stone or pizza steel
- Pizza peel

1 Remove the prepared dough from the refrigerator 2 hours before cooking.

2 Preheat the oven to 500°F (260°C) and place your pizza stone or pizza steel in the middle of the oven.

3 Place the dough ball on a floured surface and roll it out into a 12"–14" circle.

4 Transfer the dough to your favorite pizza peel, then top with the passata, a pinch of salt, and the cheese rounds (leaving a ½" lip around the edge). Lightly brush the outer crust with olive oil.

5 Slide the pizza onto the pizza stone or pizza steel and bake it for 9–13 minutes or until golden and puffy. Garnish with the basil, cut, and enjoy!

Inspiration:
A classic by Auggie Russo. Note his spacing of the cheese, allowing for some of the sauce to be exposed to the heat and caramelize.

Fig and Prosciutto Pie

The pie that made me a mega fan of Tiny Pizza Kitchen is Chef Auggie Russo's Fig and Pig, a harmony of sweet and salty flavors. The recipe below is our at-home tribute to his classic pie (which is probably worth the visit to Brooklyn alone). His version features house-preserved lemons, wine-soaked sheep's milk cheese, and dried rose petals (among other ingredients)—all of which speaks to the sheer creativity Auggie brings to the table. Our version might not be as ambitious, but we've tried to emulate the high notes of his creation. Note the use of many different cheeses, all adding to the depth of umami and tangy flavors in this pizza.

Those crispy prosciutto bits are everything in both the savory and salty flavor mix and the pop of texture they provide.

■ **Inspiration:** The even layering of Chef Auggie's prosciutto is a must here—it lets the slices melt into the pie.

- Neo-Neopolitan dough, see page 47
- 3 ounces fig preserves
- 3 ounces fresh mozzarella cheese, sliced into ½" thick rounds and patted dry
- 3 ounces goat cheese
- 2 tablespoons Romano cheese
- 2 tablespoons olive oil
- 2 tablespoons thinly sliced scallions
- 2 ounces thinly sliced prosciutto

Equipment
- Pizza stone or pizza steel
- Pizza peel

1 Remove the prepared dough from the refrigerator 2 hours before cooking.

2 Preheat the oven to 500°F (260°C) and place your pizza stone or pizza steel in the middle of the oven.

3 Place the dough ball on a floured surface and roll it out into a 12"–14" circle.

4 Transfer the dough to your favorite pizza peel, then top with the fig preserves, fresh mozzarella, goat cheese, and Romano. Drizzle the pie with olive oil.

5 Slide the pizza onto the pizza stone or pizza steel and bake it for 10–14 minutes or until just charred and puffy. Remove the pizza from the oven and top with the scallions and layer on the prosciutto.

California-Style

The California-style pizza is extremely similar to the neo-Neapolitan: both are smaller, cooked hot and fast, and include simple yet powerful toppings. In fact, many argue that the California-style is not a regional variant at all, because the dough, sauce, etc., can wildly vary. What sets this style apart is less the dough and more the toppings; if you can dream it, it is a pizza. In short, California-style pizza is more of a mindset than a recipe. The dough below is, in fact, a modified Neapolitan recipe (though the added oil and sugar help with the crust char). This pizza also benefits from a pizza stone, though the 10" size just happens to fit great on an upside-down 12" cast-iron skillet.

CALIFORNIA-STYLE DOUGH

MAKES TWO 9" TO 10" PIZZAS

Ingredients
- 1½ cups (200g) **bread flour**
- ½ cup (120mL) **of water**
- 1 teaspoon (4g) **sugar**
- 1 teaspoon (3g) **instant yeast**
- ½ teaspoon (3g) **table salt**
- 1 tablespoon (14g) **olive oil**

1 In your stand mixer or a large bowl, combine the water, sugar, yeast, flour, salt, and oil in that order. Gently mix on low or knead for 6–8 minutes.

2 Divide the dough into two equal balls, cover with plastic wrap, and let rise on the counter for 4 hours.

3 After the dough has risen, punch it down and reroll it, then move it into the refrigerator for 48 hours.

4 On pizza day, remove the dough from the refrigerator 2 hours before cooking.

Gluten-Free Alternative

Gluten-free? Try making any of the California pizzas with one batch of the gluten-free Napoletana dough on page 31. This should make two 12" or three 10" pizzas. Follow the instructions in the gluten-free Neapolitan recipe on page 39.

California

California Margherita

I don't know if there's a pizzaiolo I've met who embodies the spirit of a California pie like Ryan Mondragon, who runs a mobile and pop-up pizzeria called Sanctuary Pizza in Turlock, California, focusing on quality ingredients first and foremost. I believe you can taste passion and love within a pizza, and Ryan's work is the living proof. We'll start exploring my favorite California-style pies with a traditional one. Ryan's version of the Margherita is where our California journey begins.

Ingredients

- California-style dough, see page 53
- ½ cup passata, divided
- 6 ounces mozzarella, shredded and divided
- 10 basil leaves, divided

Equipment

- Pizza stone, pizza steel, or 12" cast-iron skillet
- Pizza peel

1 Remove the prepared dough from the refrigerator 2 hours before cooking.

2 Preheat the oven to 500°F (260°C) and place your pizza stone, pizza steel, or cast-iron skillet in the middle of the oven.

3 Place one dough ball on a floured surface and roll it out into a 9"–10" circle with a slight lip.

4 Transfer the dough to your favorite pizza peel, then top it with half the passata and half the cheese (leaving a ½" lip around the edge).

5 Slide the pizza onto the pizza stone, pizza steel, or cast-iron skillet and bake it for 8–10 minutes or until golden and puffy. Top with half the basil.

6 Repeat steps 3 through 5 with the second dough ball and the remaining toppings to create a second pizza.

Our take on the California classic Margherita; the floral basil, fruity tomatoes, and creamy cheese will have you imagining that you are on a California farm.

Inspiration:
Each of Chef Ryan Mondragon's dough bubbles is just pure textural bliss. They're shatteringly crisp to eat, which contrasts with the toppings and chewy base crust.

Cup and Char Pepperoni California

Cup and char–style pepperoni is one of the greatest foods on this planet when treated correctly. A more artisanal variant of pepperoni, the name comes from the shape it takes when cooked, forming mini bowls that are crisp at the edges and just chewy in the center. This dichotomy of textures pairs with the playful nature of the California style perfectly, also creating a visual masterpiece in the process.

Ingredients

- California-style dough, see page 53
- ½ cup passata, divided
- 8 ounces mozzarella, divided
- 6 ounces cup and char pepperoni, divided
- 10 basil leaves, divided

Equipment

- Pizza stone, pizza steel, or 12" cast-iron skillet
- Pizza peel

1 Remove the prepared dough from the refrigerator 2 hours before cooking.

2 Preheat the oven to 500°F (260°C) and place your pizza stone, pizza steel, or cast-iron skillet in the middle of the oven.

3 Place one dough ball on a floured surface and roll it out into a 9"–10" circle with a slight lip.

4 Transfer the dough to your favorite pizza peel, then top it with half the passata and cheese (leaving a ½" lip around the edge). Then add half the pepperoni.

5 Slide the pizza onto the pizza stone, pizza steel, or cast-iron skillet and bake it for 8–10 minutes or until golden and puffy. Top with the basil.

6 Repeat steps 3 through 5 with the second dough ball and the remaining toppings to create a second pizza.

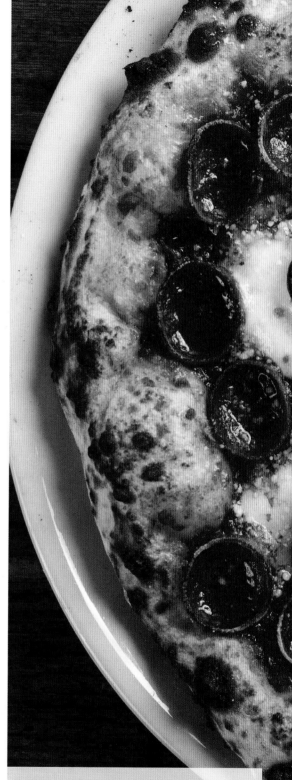

The secret to this pie is just covering the pizza in pepperoni, which of course adds flavor but also a crunchy top layer, making for the ultimate in textural experience. The flavors work well with or without the basil's fresh kick.

■ *Inspiration:*
I'm perpetually in
awe of the texture
Ryan Mondragon
achieves with his
pizzas. The cup
and char pepperoni
with the charred
crust has a range of
crispy textures that
is sublime.

BBQ Chicken

The BBQ chicken pizza is probably the most famous California-style pie, both because it is the one that put the style on the map and because of the comparative uniqueness of the toppings. Note the lower temperature used here—we want the BBQ sauce to just caramelize. At high temperatures it can burn very easily. Lowering by a few degrees is a bit of insurance that firms up the crust a bit more as well.

Note the crispier crust that results from the longer cook time. It's a welcome foil for the saucy pie—the added texture plays well with the sticky BBQ sauce, holding up until the last bite.

Ingredients
- California-style dough, see page 53
- ⅓ cup BBQ sauce, divided
- 3 ounces mozzarella, shredded and divided
- 3 ounces gouda, shredded and divided
- ¼ cup thinly sliced red onion, divided
- ½ cup cooked chicken, divided

Equipment
- Pizza stone, pizza steel, or 12" cast-iron skillet
- Pizza peel

1 Remove the prepared dough from the refrigerator 2 hours before cooking.

2 Preheat the oven to 450°F (230°C) and place your pizza stone, pizza steel, or cast-iron skillet in the middle of the oven.

3 Place one dough ball on a floured surface and roll it out into a 9"–10" circle.

4 Transfer the dough to your favorite pizza peel, then top it with half the BBQ sauce, cheeses, chicken, and red onion.

5 Slide the pizza onto the pizza stone, pizza steel, or cast-iron skillet and bake it for 10–12 minutes or until charred and wonderfully golden.

6 Repeat steps 3 through 5 with the second dough ball and the remaining toppings to create a second pizza.

New Haven

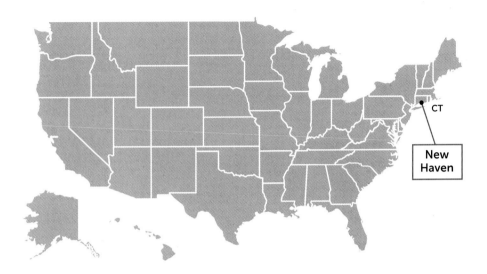

CT

New Haven

The New Haven *apizza* (pronounced "a-beetz") is like a classic Neapolitan pizza, if the chef only had a charcoal grill and lived on a New England pier. Note the long cold fermentation of the dough, which produces a very tangy and chewy dough that flourishes over the coal flame. My all-time favorite New Haven pizza hails from Pepe's (Frank Pepe Pizzeria Napoletana), widely considered to be one of the original and best apizza makers on the planet. Established in 1925 on Wooster Street by Frank and Filomena Pepe, their approach is simple: "the best ingredients on the best dough, every time." Their sauce consists of Italian tomatoes grown exclusively for Frank Pepe's (they use the same tomatoes at every location). The business is still owned by the Pepe family, currently Frank Pepe's grandchildren. They have kept the same ingredients and process that Frank used in 1925, including the use of a coal-fired oven, which gives their pizza the iconic char and crispy yet chewy crust.

NEW HAVEN DOUGH

MAKES ONE 12" TO 14" PIZZA

Ingredients

- 1½ cups (200g) **bread flour**
- ½ cup (130mL) **water, plus a splash**
- 1 teaspoon (3g) **active dry yeast**
- ¾ teaspoon (4.5g) **table salt**

1 In the work bowl of your stand mixer, dissolve the yeast in the water. Add in the flour and salt. Using the hook attachment, mix for 8 minutes on low speed.

2 Form the dough into a ball, cover it, and let the dough rise on the counter for 4 hours.

3 Following this rise, punch down, then proof for 24–48 hours in the refrigerator.

4 On pizza day, remove the dough from the refrigerator 2 hours before cooking.

New Haven White Clam

The white clam pie was created in the 1960s and is a thin Neapolitan-style pizza (the dough is nearly identical). The similarities end there, as it is cooked over a charcoal fire and topped either with clams (which makes perfect sense given where apizza was invented) or a scant amount of cheese. This clam pie, then, is an homage to Pepe's version, one of the most unique and flavorful pizzas in this entire book.

Ingredients

- New Haven dough, see page 59
- ⅓ cup chopped clams, drained
- ¼ cup grated Pecorino Romano
- 1 teaspoon dried oregano
- 2 cloves garlic, minced
- ½ teaspoon freshly ground black pepper
- 1 ounce bacon, cooked and chopped
- Extra-virgin olive oil, for drizzling

Equipment

- 14" pizza pan
- Charcoal grill or gas grill*

If you're using a gas grill, just place a few charcoal chunks under the grates when you preheat to ensure that authentic flavor with less fuss. Aim for the same temperatures and cooking times.

1 Remove the prepared dough from the refrigerator 2 hours before cooking.

2 Build a charcoal fire in your grill, aiming for medium heat. Remove any upper racks, and ensure the grates are spotless (any little bits will burn). The target temperature is 500°F (260°C), with indirect heat in the middle (the pizza cooking area) as much as possible.

3 As the grill heats, press out your pizza dough. Your goal is a 14" circle with a slight lip around the edge.

4 Place the dough on your pan, and top your pizza with the clams, Pecorino Romano, oregano, garlic, and pepper, leaving ½" lip around the edge.

5 Place the pan onto the grill and cook for 6–8 minutes until the crust is set. Finish the pizza directly on the grates for 1–2 minutes to get that signature char. Remove the pizza from the grill, drizzle it with olive oil, and finish with the bacon. Cut and serve!

If you didn't harvest your own clams this morning, store-bought will be fine.

Inspiration: The briny clams against the tangy Pecorino Romano in Pepe's legendary pairing shines when cooked on the smoky grill or oven.

A-Beetz

The other classic New Haven pie is the A-Beetz. This pizza is somewhere between a classic cheese and a tomato pie, where the dough and sauce are the stars. The Pecorino Romano cheese adds a salty, tangy flavor that shines against the charred crust and sweet tomatoes. Our version keeps the same theme: Pecorino Romano, tomatoes, and a fire-kissed crust. I promise you won't miss the mozzarella one bit.

That wood-fired crust is everything, giving a smoky charred flavor to the garlicky sauce.

■ **Inspiration:** Pronounced "a-beetz," Pepe's apizza is a New Haven classic, where the fruity and garlic-forward tomato sauce is the star.

Ingredients
- New Haven dough, see page 59
- ⅔ cup passata or tomato puree
- 1 teaspoon dried oregano
- ½ teaspoon salt
- 3 tablespoons grated Pecorino Romano
- Extra-virgin olive oil, for drizzling

Equipment
- 14" pizza pan
- Charcoal grill or gas grill*

*If you're using a gas grill, just place a few charcoal chunks under the grates when you preheat to ensure that authentic flavor with less fuss. Aim for the same temperatures and cooking times.

1 Remove the prepared dough from the refrigerator 2 hours before cooking.

2 Build a charcoal fire in your grill, aiming for medium heat. Remove any upper racks, and ensure the grates are spotless (any little bits will burn). The target temperature is 500°F (260°C).

3 As the grill heats, press out your pizza dough. Your goal is a 14" circle with a slight lip around the edge.

4 Place the dough on your pan, and top your pizza with the passata, oregano, salt, and Pecorino Romano.

5 Place the pan onto the grill and cook for 6–8 minutes until the crust is set. Finish the pizza directly on the grates for 1–2 minutes to get that signature char. Remove the pizza from the grill, drizzle it with olive oil, cut, and serve!

A-Mootz

A-Mootz is the New Haven version of the classic cheese pie ("mootz" = mozzarella), though it doesn't have as much cheese as a New York slice. Again, the grill and the dough do the culinary heavy lifting here, with the cheese providing a gentle backdrop.

■ **Inspiration:** High heat makes for the crispiest pizza crust in Pepe's original.

This pizza has more cheese than the A-Beetz, shifting the flavors from a sharp sweetness to a more traditional cheesy bite.

Ingredients
- New Haven dough, see page 59
- ⅔ cup passata or tomato puree
- 1 teaspoon dried oregano
- ¼ teaspoon salt
- 2 ounces mozzarella, grated
- 3 tablespoons grated Pecorino Romano
- Extra-virgin olive oil, for drizzling

Equipment
- 14" pizza pan
- Charcoal grill or gas grill*

If you're using a gas grill, just place a few charcoal chunks under the grates when you preheat to ensure that authentic flavor with less fuss. Aim for the same temperatures and cooking times.

1 Remove the prepared dough from the refrigerator 2 hours before cooking.

2 Build a charcoal fire in your grill, aiming for medium heat. Remove any upper racks, and ensure the grates are spotless (any little bits will burn). The target temperature is 500°F (260°C).

3 As the grill heats, press out your pizza dough. Your goal is a 14" circle with a slight lip around the edge.

4 Place the dough on your pan, and top your pizza with the passata, oregano, salt, mozzarella, and Pecorino Romano.

5 Place the pan onto the grill and cook for 6–8 minutes until the crust is set. Finish the pizza directly on the grates for 1–2 minutes to get that signature char. Remove the pizza from the grill, drizzle it with olive oil, cut, and serve!

Montanara

One of the most underrated styles in this book, the Montanara pizza, which is lightly fried then baked to doneness, is wonderfully delicate and light despite being fried. Hailing from Naples, this style of pizza is truly a piece of art when properly prepared, and not at all heavy. Note the very simple dough recipe, which is very close to the traditional Neapolitan. This style is also great for make-ahead purposes; fry the pizzas and hold them until service, then finish them as needed.

MONTANARA DOUGH

MAKES FOUR 10" PIZZAS

Ingredients
- 3½ cups (472g) **bread flour**
- 1¼ cups (312mL) **water**
- 1½ teaspoons (9g) **table salt**
- 1 teaspoon (3g) **active dry yeast**

1 In the work bowl of your stand mixer, gently combine the flour, salt, and yeast.

2 Attach the dough hook, turn the stand mixer on low, and slowly add the water. Mix for 4 minutes.

3 Remove the dough and knead it on the board for another 2–3 minutes. Once smooth, form the dough into a rough ball and let it sit at room temperature overnight.

4 Once the dough has risen, punch it down and divide it into four pieces. Form the pieces into balls, cover them, and let them rest for 2 hours before cooking.

Naples, Italy

Montanara Marinara

We will start with a simple marinara (tomato sauce and hard cheese only) to get our culinary feet wet on this style of pie. This recipe makes four 10" pizzas, which is perfect for a party (and to fit into a Dutch oven for frying).

This is a deceptively light and airy pizza, not greasy as one would expect from the frying.

Ingredients

- Montanara dough, see page 64
- 1 cup passata, divided
- 2 ounces Parmigiano-Reggiano, divided
- Fresh basil leaves, divided

Equipment

- 2 quarts neutral oil, for frying
- Large Dutch oven, for frying
- Oven
- Pizza pan, optional

1 Once the dough balls have rested for 2 hours, roll them out into four 8"–10" circles that are ¼" thick.

2 Heat the frying oil in a large Dutch oven to 350°F (175°C). Fry one pizza for 90 seconds, then remove it from the oil and set it aside on a draining rack. Fry the other three pizzas.

3 Once the pizzas are fried, preheat the oven to 475°F (245°C). Top each pizza with a quarter of the passata and Parmigiano-Reggiano.

4 Bake the pizzas directly on the rack or on a pizza pan for 4–5 minutes to melt the cheese and finish the dough. Once cooked, garnish with the basil leaves and serve.

Montanara Margherita Pizza

Don Antonio in Manhattan serves some of the finest pizza on the planet. Run by World Champion, revered teacher, and renowned pizzaiola Giorgia Caporuscio, their pies are truly world class. Here, she uses the finest ingredients to create utter culinary magic. One of her signature pies is, of course, the Montanara pizza. Never greasy, always satisfying, Giorgia's is one of the best examples of this style of pizza. Our tribute to her classic is a play on the Margherita pizza, set against the Montanara backdrop.

Look at the height that's achieved when frying—this creates an airy bite that is almost like a savory cloud.

Inspiration:
Giorgia Caporuscio's pizzas are just beautiful. She creates the most wonderful texture on her crust.

Ingredients
- Montanara dough, see page 64
- 1 cup passata, divided
- 8 ounces fresh mozzarella, sliced and divided
- Fresh basil leaves, divided

Equipment
- 2 quarts neutral oil, for frying
- Large Dutch oven, for frying
- Oven
- Pizza pan, optional

1 Once the dough balls have rested for 2 hours, roll them out into four 8"–10" circles that are ¼" thick.

2 Heat the frying oil in a large Dutch oven to 350°F (175°C). Fry one pizza for 90 seconds, then remove it from the oil and set it aside on a draining rack. Fry the other three pizzas.

3 Once the pizzas are fried, preheat the oven to 475°F (245°C). Top each pizza with a quarter of the passata and mozzarella.

4 Bake the pizzas directly on the rack or on a pizza pan for 4–5 minutes to melt the cheese and finish the dough. Once cooked, garnish with the basil leaves and serve.

Elephant Ears

The most dramatic transition we will have in this book is from legendary Italian pizzas to standard American fair fare. Elephant ears are a classic for good reason, and, with slight modification, our Montanara dough can turn into an epic at-home dessert. While this recipe calls for cinnamon sugar, feel free to top with whatever your inner 10-year-old desires.

You can also top this with powdered sugar, apple pie filling, or chocolate sauce. The world is your elephant ear.

Ingredients
- Montanara dough, see page 64
- ¼ cup cinnamon sugar, divided

Equipment
- 2 quarts neutral oil, for frying
- Large Dutch oven, for frying
- Oven
- Pizza pan, optional

1 Once the dough balls have rested for 2 hours, roll them out into four 8"–10" circles that are ¼" thick.

2 Heat the frying oil in a large Dutch oven to 350°F (175°C). Fry one elephant ear for 90 seconds, then remove it from the oil and set it aside on a draining rack. Fry the other three elephant ears.

3 Increase the heat on the oil to 375°F (175°C) and refry one ear for 30–40 second or until just brown on the edges. Remove it from the oil and set it aside on a draining rack. Cover it with one-quarter of the cinnamon sugar.

4 Refry and add cinnamon sugar to the other three elephant ears.

Pan *Style*

Pan pizza is a style based less on the dough and more on the cooking vessel itself, offering a crispy, golden crust that's thicker than most traditional pizzas. Here, a high-walled pan is critical for the structure of the pizza, allowing the dough to grow and set in the pan. Characterized by its high, oft-caramelized edges and satisfying crunch, pan pizza combines a rich texture with thick slices that are unmistakably indulgent. This style is often defined by a cooking technique that involves plenty of oil in the pan, which contributes to its unique crust that almost fries while baking. In this section, we'll explore a variety of pan pizza styles, starting with the iconic Chicago deep dish and its cousin, the Chicago stuffed pizza. We'll journey through the caramelized edges of Detroit-style pizza and the unique twists of Colorado and Cuban pizzas. Finally, we'll wrap up with the versatile and delicious variants of the calzone.

Pan pizzas, often featuring crispy crusts and fluffy interiors, are both user-friendly and wildly rewarding to make.

Classic Pan

Pan pizzas are amazingly satisfying to both craft and eat. The use of a pan certainly varies in the pizza landscape, from the use of deep-dish round pans, cast-iron skillets, specialty Detroit pans, and sheet pans. Here, we'll start with the classic pan crust—crispy, fluffy perfection.

CLASSIC PAN DOUGH

MAKES ONE 12" PIZZA

Ingredients
- 1½ cups (200g) **bread flour**
- ⅓ cup (79mL) **water**
- ¼ cup (59mL) **milk**
- ½ teaspoon (2g) **sugar**
- 1 teaspoon (3g) **instant yeast**
- ¾ teaspoon (4.5g) **table salt**
- 1 tablespoon (28g) **vegetable oil, plus more for the pan**

1 In your stand mixer or large bowl, gently combine the water, milk, sugar, and yeast. Let stand for 5 minutes.

2 Following the rest period, mix on low with the hook attachment or with your hands.

3 Gently pour in the flour, salt, and oil. Mix for 6 minutes on medium-low speed, then form the dough into a ball.

4 Transfer the dough to a large, greased bowl and let it rise for 4 hours. Then transfer it to the fridge and let it rise as long as overnight, punching it down once.

5 Bring the dough to room temperature 2 hours before cooking.

CLASSIC PAN SAUCE

MAKES ONE 12" PIZZA

Ingredients
- 1 tablespoon **olive oil**
- ¾ cup **crushed tomatoes**
- 1 clove **garlic, crushed**
- ¼ teaspoon **dried oregano**
- 1 pinch **salt**

1 Place a saucepot over low heat and add in the olive oil, crushed tomatoes, garlic, oregano, and salt.

2 Bring the mixture to a simmer and cook for 5 minutes on low.

3 Cool and set aside in the refrigerator for future use.

Gluten-Free Alternative

Gluten-free flour, due to its specific makeup, requires a much higher hydration ratio than traditional doughs. In some instances, this can make the dough a bit more temperamental to deal with. With pan styles, you can use the pan to make the process go more smoothly. I use Caputo Fioreglut Gluten Free Flour, because I find it to be the closest to traditional flour and the easiest to work with. Feel free to use your favorite GF flour, just note that some trial and error will be needed. See page 75 for a full recipe using the gluten-free classic pan dough. **Note:** The gluten-free classic pan dough can also be used to make some of the Sicilian-style pizzas.

GLUTEN-FREE CLASSIC PAN DOUGH

MAKES ONE 12" PIZZA

Ingredients

- **3 cups** (272g) **Caputo Fioreglut Gluten Free Flour**
- **1 cup** (225g) **water, warmed to 100°F** (38°C)
- **1 teaspoon** (6g) **salt**
- **2 teaspoons** (6g) **instant yeast**
- **2 teaspoons** (11g) **olive oil**

1 In the work bowl of your stand mixer, combine the water, yeast, and olive oil.

2 Slowly add in the flour and salt and work on low using the hook attachment for 5 to 10 minutes.

3 Cover and let the dough rise for 1 to 2 hours.

4 When the dough has about doubled, gently form it into the shape of your particular pan, grease the pan and move the dough into the pan. Cover it and let it rise for 2 hours.

Classic Pan Pizza

Remember when you were a kid, and there was that program where you could read a few books and get a pizza in return? This is that pizza. A crisp, fluffy, slightly greasy (in the *best* way) pan pizza that will make you want a pitcher of soda and some quarters for the arcade. And since the chain restaurant in question invented the pan pizza (in Kansas, of all places, in 1959), it's only fitting to write a recipe in homage to the original. If you are bold enough, instead of greasing the pan with olive oil, use a tablespoon of butter-flavored shortening for a more "classic" taste.

Bonus points if served alongside a red plastic cup on a checkered tablecloth.

Ingredients
- Classic pan pizza dough, see page 70
- Classic pan pizza sauce, see page 70
- 6 ounces mozzarella cheese, grated
- 2 tablespoons Parmesan, plus more for finishing

Equipment
- Olive oil for greasing
- 12" cast-iron skillet or lipped pizza pan

> You can also use this recipe to make two smaller 8" pizzas, should you want to reward yourself for a great report card or completed reading list. Lower the cook time to 10–12 minutes each and use your favorite 8" metal cooking vessel.

1 Bring the dough to room temperature 2 hours before cooking.

2 Preheat the oven to 475°F (245°C) and move a rack to the lower third of the oven. Grease the pan liberally with the olive oil.

3 Move the dough onto a floured surface and form it into a 10"–12" circle.

4 Move the dough into the pan, pressing it into the sides to form the crust lip. Let it rise in the pan for another 30–60 minutes.

5 Top the pizza with the sauce and cheeses, leaving a ½" border of crust all around. Finish with additional Parmesan.

6 Bake the pizza for 14–16 minutes or until deeply golden. Transfer to a cutting board, cut into slices, and devour.

Stuffed Crust

Yeah, I know what you're thinking—you want a stuffed crust pie now. I got you. The secret here, quite literally, is in the crust. Take your time with this one, being sure to fully seal the cheese sticks in the dough. When you get more proficient with the maneuver, feel free to throw some garlic butter in with the stuffed cheese.

Feel free to eat this crust-first just like we did in the 1990s. The gooey cheese in the crust is the best part, after all!

Ingredients
- Classic pan pizza dough, see page 70
- Classic pan pizza sauce, see page 70
- 3 white string cheese sticks
- 1 tablespoon cornstarch
- 8 ounces mozzarella, grated
- 2 tablespoons Parmesan
- 3 ounces pepperoni

Equipment
- Olive oil for greasing
- 12" cast-iron skillet or lipped pizza pan

1 Prepare the string cheese by tearing each piece lengthwise into thirds. Place the cheese in the freezer for 2 hours. Bring the dough to room temperature 2 hours before cooking.

2 Preheat the oven to 475°F (245°C) and move a rack to the lower third of the oven. Grease the pan with the olive oil.

3 Roll out the dough into a 14" circle and move it into the greased pan. Press the dough into the sides to form the crust lip. As you form the lip, coat each piece of cheese with cornstarch and slide it into the space where the dough hits the corner of the pan. Fold the dough over and repeat.

4 Let the dough rise in the pan for an hour. (This will take care of any tears or seams.)

5 Top the pizza with the sauce, mozzarella, Parmesan, and pepperoni.

6 Bake the pizza for 14–16 minutes or until deeply golden and charred around the edges. Once cooked, use a butter knife to free the pizza from the sides of the pan (in case of cheese oozing from the crust). Transfer to a cutting board, cut into slices, and devour.

Caramelized Cheese Crust

My favorite pan pizzas have a lip of caramelized cheese around the outside, creating a wonderful mix of textures. Borrowing guidance from Chicago Stuffed and Cuban pizzas (see pages 82 and 106), we can create an outstanding pie.

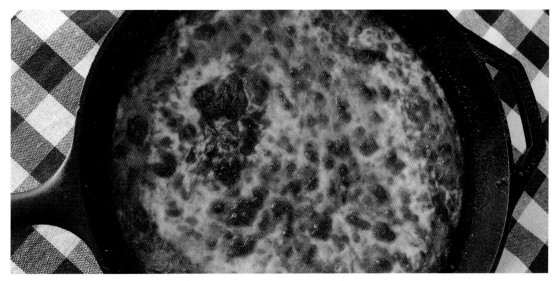

That cheese isn't burnt, it's caramelized and ready to eat.

Ingredients

- Classic pan pizza dough, see page 70
- Classic pan pizza sauce, see page 70
- 6 ounces mozzarella, grated
- 4 ounces white cheddar, grated
- 2 ounces provolone, sliced and cut into 1" strips
- 2 tablespoons grated Parmesan

Equipment

- Olive oil for greasing
- 12" cast-iron skillet or lipped pizza pan

1 Bring the dough to room temperature 2 hours before cooking.

2 Preheat the oven to 475°F (245°C) and move a rack to the lower third of the oven. Grease the pan liberally with the olive oil.

3 Move the dough onto a floured surface and form it into a 12" circle.

4 Move the dough into the pan, pressing it into the sides to form the crust lip. Let it rise in the pan for another 30–60 minutes.

5 Top the pizza with the sauce, mozzarella, and white cheddar, pushing both cheeses right out to the edge. Press the sliced provolone into the sides of the pan, then top everything with the Parmesan.

6 Bake the pizza for 14–16 minutes or until deeply golden and charred around the edges. Transfer to a cutting board, cut into slices, and devour.

GF Pan

For a gluten-free pan crust, we can use the pan to do a lot of the hard work for us, making a wonderful slice that rivals any in this book. If you don't have a 12" x 10" pizza pan to use for this classic Margherita, use a cast-iron skillet to create equally awesome results!

So crisp and so light, the specific flour I recommend makes for a very pleasing structure in the crumb of the pizza.

Ingredients
- Gluten-free classic pan pizza dough, see page 71
- Classic pan pizza sauce, see page 70
- 6 ounces mozzarella, grated
- 2 tablespoons grated Parmesan, plus more for finishing

Equipment
- Olive oil for greasing
- 12" x 10" pizza pan or 12" cast-iron skillet

1 Prepare the dough and the sauce.

2 Preheat the oven to 475°F (245°C) and move a rack to the lower third of the oven. Grease the pan liberally with the olive oil.

3 Following the bench proof, top the pizza with the sauce and the cheeses, leaving a ½" border of crust all around. Finish with additional Parmesan.

4 Bake the pizza for 14–16 minutes or until golden around the edges. Transfer to a cutting board, cut into slices, and devour.

Chicago Deep Dish

Chicago-style deep-dish and stuffed-crust pizzas are borderline controversial outside of the Midwest. Admittedly, these pies are closer to a casserole than most other pizzas, but make no mistake, they belong on the Mount Rushmore of Pizza (which, 10/10, would visit).

Deep-dish pizza, with the upside-down construction of cheese, toppings, then sauce, has a signature flakiness in the crust and sweetness in the tomato sauce, plus that ½" layer of cheese. In fact, this is one of the only doughs that has both oil and butter in it, closer to a pot pie dough than a pizza (but it's still pizza). Personally, it's the slight caramelization of the tomato layer that makes this pie—the sauce becomes ever-so-sticky in the best way.

CHICAGO DEEP DISH DOUGH

MAKES ONE 12" PIZZA

Ingredients

- 3¼ cups (390g) **all-purpose flour**
- 1 cup (237mL) **water, warmed to 100°F (38°C)**
- 2 teaspoons (8g) **sugar**
- 2 teaspoons (6g) **active dry yeast**
- 1½ teaspoons (9g) **table salt**
- 1 pinch **cream of tartar**
- 3 tablespoons (42g) **corn oil**
- 3 tablespoons (45g) **melted butter**

1 In the work bowl of your stand mixer, combine the sugar, yeast, and water, along with 1 cup of the flour. Let rest for 5 minutes.

2 Add in the remaining flour and the salt, cream of tartar, corn oil, and melted butter. Knead on low using the hook attachment for 5 minutes.

3 Form the dough into a ball and move it to a nonstick, spray-oiled bowl. Let it rise on the counter for 4–6 hours, punching it down once.

CHICAGO PAN DOUGH

MAKES ONE 12" PIZZA

Ingredients

- 1½ cups (200g) **bread flour**
- ½ cup plus 1 tablespoon (130mL) **water**
- ½ teaspoon (2g) **sugar**
- 1 teaspoon (3g) **active dry yeast**
- ¾ teaspoon (4g) **table salt**
- 1 tablespoon (14g) **olive oil**

1 In the work bowl of your stand mixer, combine the sugar, yeast, and water, along with 1 cup of the flour. Let rest for 5 minutes.

2 Add in the remaining flour and the salt and olive oil. Knead on low using the hook attachment for 5 minutes.

3 Form the dough into a ball and move it to a nonstick, spray-oiled bowl. Let it rise on the counter for 4–6 hours, punching it down once.

4 Remove the dough from the fridge two hours before planning to roll.

Chicago

IL

Gluten-Free Alternative

Along with the gluten-free classic pan dough on page 71, deep-dish pizzas work very well with gluten-free cauliflower dough. Again, the pan helps provide structure. I often use Caputo Fioreglut Gluten Free Flour, because I find it to be the closest to traditional flour and the easiest to work with, but it's not as critical in this recipe as in the other gluten-free dough recipes. Feel free to use your favorite GF flour, just note that some trial and error will be needed. See page 70 for a full recipe using the cauliflower pizza dough.

CAULIFLOWER PIZZA DOUGH

MAKES ONE 12" PIZZA

Ingredients

- 4 cups (400g) riced cauliflower (frozen, steam-in-bag preferred)
- 2 eggs
- 1 clove garlic
- ½ cup (113g) grated Parmesan
- 3 tablespoons (17g) Caputo Fioreglut Gluten Free Flour
- ½ teaspoon (3g) salt
- ¼ teaspoon (0.6g) black pepper

1 Preheat the oven to 400°F (205°C). Cook the riced cauliflower per the package directions or steam for 6 minutes, then squeeze out any excess moisture using a tea towel or cheesecloth.

2 In a food processor, combine the eggs, riced cauliflower, garlic, Parmesan cheese, gluten-free flour, salt, and pepper. Process until a batter-like consistency forms, adjusting with more gluten-free flour if needed.

3 Thoroughly grease the skillet with olive oil, then mold the cauliflower batter into the bottom and sides of the pan, ensuring it covers the sides without protruding.

4 Blind bake the crust for 15 minutes until it becomes just golden, then continue adding toppings and complete the final bake.

Classic Deep Dish with Sausage

One note for these pizzas: most recipes call for raw sausage, including this one. The grease from the sausage essentially fries the pizza from the inside out, and it just cannot be fully substituted, which is why this base recipe recommends it. At a cook time of over 30 minutes, I've never had an issue with the temperature of the pizza reaching 170°F (75°C), but if you are worried about this or want to keep it vegetarian, either swap the sausage for pepperoni or give the toppings you do use a nice swirl of olive oil.

Look at that cheese pull with the layer of sausage behind it. Spicy, cheesy, and a little sweet from the tomato layer, this is a much more complex slice than meets the eye.

Ingredients

- Chicago deep dish dough, see page 76
- 1 cup whole canned tomatoes
- 1 teaspoon dried oregano
- ½ teaspoon salt
- 12 ounces mozzarella, sliced thin
- 8 ounces bulk sweet Italian sausage
- 2 tablespoons grated Parmesan

Equipment

- 3 tablespoons butter
- 12" x 1½" pizza pan or 12" cast-iron skillet

1 Before pizza day, prepare the tomatoes by straining off any juice and gently crushing them. Combine them with the oregano and salt, then store them until you're ready to cook.

2 Earlier in the day, prepare the dough.

3 Once the dough has risen, preheat the oven to 450°F (230°C).

4 Punch down the dough and roll it into a 16" circle that is ⅓"–½" thick. Rub the pan with the butter, then lay the dough into the pan, being sure to run the dough lip up to the very edge. Trim any excess dough (there will be some).

5 Top the pizza in this order: slices of mozzarella, raw sausage, tomatoes, and grated Parmesan.

6 Bake for 25–30 minutes, rotating once. The pizza is done when the crust is deeply golden, and the internal temperature is 175°F (80°C). (Be sure to check to ensure the sausage is properly cooked.)

Cauliflower Deep Dish

Not just a gimmick, this cauliflower deep-dish pizza produces a wonderfully cheesy pizza that has a crust that holds up to the toppings and sauce. A great pizza main or an unforgettable side for a holiday party (hence the Christmas tree cheese design), you'll totally dig this veggie-crust pizza!

Perfect as a holiday side, or as a changeup to a traditional deep-dish pizza.

Ingredients

- Cauliflower pizza dough, see page 77
- 2 pints cherry tomatoes
- 2 tablespoons olive oil
- 1 pound Italian sausage, cooked and crumbled
- 10 ounces mozzarella, sliced
- ½ cup grated Parmesan

Equipment

- 12" cast-iron skillet

1 Preheat the oven to 400°F (205°C). Prepare and blind bake the cauliflower pizza dough.

2 In a separate baking pan, combine the cherry tomatoes, olive oil, and a pinch of salt. Bake in the same oven for 6–8 minutes or until blistered.

3 Once the crust is blind baked and the tomatoes are blistered, heat the oven to 450°F (230°C). Layer on the crust a third of the mozzarella cheese, followed by the sausage and then the remaining mozzarella. Add the baked tomatoes and top with the Parmesan cheese.

4 Bake for 20–25 minutes or until the cheese is bubbly. Serve immediately.

Burnt Cheese with Pepper and Sausage

There is no shortage of fine deep-dish pizzas in Chicago. For me, when I think of true Chicago deep-dish or pan pizza, Burt's Place is at the top of the list. The original owner, Burt Katz, was the creator of the former Chicago pizza institution Gulliver's Pizza and the current institution Pequod's Pizza. In 1989, he founded Burt's Place, which is still crafting world-class pies to this day. Now owned by Jerry Petrow, Burt's makes a deep dish with a thicker, lighter crust, more akin to a pan pizza. Additionally, these pies have a slight rim of burnt cheese around the crust. We can make something similar at home, though we will slightly change up the dough from Burt's to better represent the lightness of this style, crossing it with a classic pan pizza recipe.

Ingredients

- Chicago pan dough, see page 76
- 1 tablespoon butter
- ½ cup sliced bell peppers
- 10 ounces mozzarella cheese, sliced
- ⅔ cup crushed tomatoes
- ¼ teaspoon dried oregano

- ¼ teaspoon salt, plus 1 pinch
- 8 ounces bulk hot Italian Sausage, cooked and crumbled
- 2 tablespoons grated Parmesan
- ½ teaspoon red pepper flakes

Equipment

- Olive oil, for the pan
- 12" x 1½" pizza pan or 12" cast-iron skillet

1 Before pizza day, prepare the bell peppers. Place a small sauté pan over medium heat and add in the tablespoon of butter and bell peppers. Sweat the peppers with a pinch of salt for 4–5 minutes. Chill them for future use.

2 Earlier in the day, prepare the dough.

3 Prepare the tomato sauce by combining the crushed tomatoes with the oregano and salt.

4 Once the dough has risen, preheat the oven to 475°F (245°C). Grease the pizza pan or cast-iron skillet liberally with the oil.

5 Move the dough onto a floured surface and form it into a 12"–14" circle. Move the dough into the pan, press it into the sides, and let it rise in the pan for another hour.

6 Following the bench proof, top the pizza with the slices of cheese, pushing the cheese right out to the pan edges. Finish with the crushed tomatoes, sausage, bell peppers, Parmesan, and red pepper flakes.

7 Bake the pizza for 16–20 minutes or until deeply golden and charred around the edges.

8 Once cooked, use a butter knife or spatula to free the pizza from the sides of the pan. Transfer to a cutting board, cut into slices, and devour.

The varying degrees of "golden brown and delicious" make this pizza. The sausage, peppers, sauce, and cheese are all cooked to perfection, yet none outshines the others.

Inspiration: The cheese crust, the charred peppers, and that wonderful sausage—this is a world-class pie from Burt's. The red-yellow-green "stoplight" peppers are a signature of Burt's, as well, lending a visual appeal and an earthy sweetness.

Chicago Stuffed

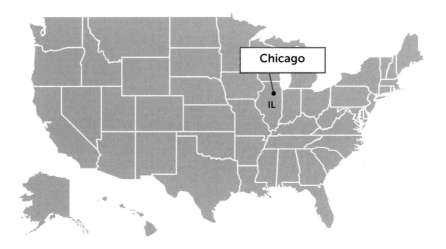

Chicago stuffed pizza is just deep dish with an extra layer of love. Made essentially the same, the difference is a layer of dough between the sauce and the cheese and toppings. This style tends to hold together a bit better once served, which is a plus. Note the longer cooking time required compared to a standard Chicago deep dish, again due to the extra dough in the middle.

STUFFED PIZZA DOUGH

MAKES ONE 12" PIZZA

Ingredients

- 3¼ cups (390g) **all-purpose flour**
- 1 cup (237mL) **water, warmed to 100°F (38°C)**
- 2 teaspoons (8g) **sugar**
- 2 teaspoons (6g) **active dry yeast**
- 1½ teaspoons (9g) **table salt**
- ⅛ teaspoon (0.4g) **cream of tartar**
- 3 tablespoons (42g) **corn oil**
- 3 tablespoons (45g) **melted butter**

1 In the work bowl of your stand mixer, combine the sugar, yeast, and water, along with 1 cup of the flour. Let rest for 5 minutes.

2 Add in the remaining flour and the salt, cream of tartar, corn oil, and melted butter. Knead on low using the hook attachment for 5 minutes.

3 Form the dough into a ball and move it to a nonstick, spray-oiled bowl. Let it rise on the counter for 2 hours, then in the refrigerator overnight.

4 Remove the dough from the fridge 2 hours before planning to roll.

Classic Stuffed with Sausage

The cousin of the Chicago deep dish, the stuffed pizza is a slight variant on the Windy City staple. It's a classic example of where the ingredients might be the same as another style, but the technique creates a very different result.

Note the subtle difference from the deep dish, with that layer of dough under the sauce holding everything together so nicely.

Ingredients
- Stuffed pizza dough, see page 82
- 1 cup whole canned tomatoes
- 1 teaspoon dried oregano
- ½ teaspoon salt
- 12 ounces mozzarella, sliced thin
- 8 ounces bulk sweet Italian sausage
- 2 tablespoons grated Parmesan

Equipment
- Nonstick spray
- 1 tablespoon melted butter
- 12" x 1½" pizza pan or 12" cast-iron skillet

1 Before pizza day, prepare the tomatoes by straining off any juice and gently crushing them. Combine them with the oregano and salt, then store them until you're ready to cook.

2 Remove the dough from the fridge 2 hours before planning to roll.

3 Preheat the oven to 450°F (230°C).

4 Punch down the dough and roll it into a 16" circle that is ⅓"–½" thick. Spray the pan liberally with nonstick spray then grease the pan with the melted butter. Lay the dough into the pan, being sure to run the dough lip up to the very edge. Trim any excess dough (there will be some).

5 Reroll the excess dough into a thin 12" circle (you should have just enough).

6 Top the pizza in this order: slices of mozzarella, raw sausage, dough circle (crimping it into the sidewall crust and making 3–4 slits in the top surface of the dough for steam to release), tomatoes, and grated Parmesan.

7 Bake for 35–40 minutes, rotating once. The pizza is done when the crust is deeply golden, and the internal temperature is 175°F (80°C).

Stuffed Supreme Pizza

Making stuffed pizza is an art. For me, no one quite masters the art like The Art of Pizza in Chicago. From The Art of Pizza:

> For over 30 years, Arthur (Art) Shabez has quietly maintained The Art of Pizza, one of Chicago's top-rated pizzerias in the Lakeview neighborhood. Art's journey in pizzeria ownership began with Coluta's Pizza in 1980, laying the foundation for his future in the Chicago pizza scene. Today, The Art of Pizza remains almost identical to its original form, a testament to Art's consistency and quality. Made with vine-ripened tomatoes, fragrant oregano and basil, and a hint of red pepper, this sauce is generously slathered over every pie, adding a burst of flavor that keeps customers [like me] coming back for more.

The Art of Pizza has become a Chicago staple, a must-visit for pizza aficionados and anyone who simply loves pizza. My favorite pie at The Art of Pizza is the Art's Special, a well-crafted supreme pizza that hits the spot every single time. Let's borrow inspiration from Art's supreme pizza and use the same veggies and sausage in our pie.

Ingredients

- Stuffed pizza dough, see page 82
- 1 tablespoon butter
- ⅓ cup sliced green bell pepper
- ⅓ cup sliced white onion
- ⅓ cup sliced button mushrooms
- 1½ cups whole canned tomatoes
- 1 teaspoon dried oregano
- ½ teaspoon salt, plus 1 pinch
- 12 ounces mozzarella, sliced thin
- 8 ounces bulk sweet Italian sausage
- 2 tablespoons grated Parmesan

Equipment

- Nonstick spray
- 12" x 1½" pizza pan or 12" cast-iron skillet

1 Before pizza day, prepare the vegetables. Place a small sauté pan over medium heat and add in the butter, green pepper, and onion (along with a pinch of salt). Sweat the veggies with a pinch of salt for 4–5 minutes. Set them aside and repeat with the mushrooms, cooking for 7–8 minutes. Strain off any juice from the tomatoes and gently crush them. Combine them with oregano and ½ teaspoon of salt. Separately chill the prepared vegetables until you're ready to cook.

2 Remove the dough from the fridge 2 hours before planning to roll.

3 Preheat the oven to 450°F (230°C).

4 Punch down the dough and roll it into a 16" circle that is ⅓"–½" thick. Spray the pan liberally with nonstick spray then grease the pan with the melted butter. Lay the dough into the pan, being sure to run the dough lip up to the very edge. Trim any excess dough (there will be some).

5 Reroll the excess dough into a thin 12" circle (you should have just enough).

6 Top the pizza in this order: slices of mozzarella, raw sausage, peppers and onions, mushrooms, dough circle (crimping it into the sidewall crust and making 3–4 slits in the top surface of the dough for steam to release), tomatoes, and grated Parmesan.

7 Bake for 35–40 minutes, rotating once. The pizza is done when the crust is deeply golden, and the internal temperature is 175°F (80°C).

This has a 10 / 10 cheese pull, which is a lot of the fun of a stuffed pizza. The extra layer of dough provides not only structure but a contrast in textures throughout the bite.

Inspiration: Art's crust is so crunchy and light, yet strong enough to support all of the wonderful toppings.

Detroit

Detroit-style pizza has its roots in Sicilian pizzas, though it has a quicker rise and a crispier texture. Created in a neighborhood bar in the 1940s, think of this pizza as a Sicilian with a deep twist (and a burnt-cheese crust). This pizza may look like a deep-dish or pan pizza, but it has a complexity one would not expect due to the use of brick cheese, a cheese somewhere between soft cheddar and mozzarella. The pan is one of the most important parts of this recipe. I have used a 9" x 13" metal baking pan with excellent results, but an authentic 10" x 14" Detroit pizza pan is the best choice. The use of corn oil is specific and authentic to some of the Detroit styles, giving a signature flavor and texture. Also note the technique here—instead of truly stretching the dough on the board, we do so in the pan to maximize the texture, given that this is a very high-hydration dough. Finally, be sure to lightly press the cheese into the sides of the pan, which will promote that iconic burnt cheese "frico" that makes Detroit-style pizza shine.

DETROIT PIZZA DOUGH

MAKES ONE 10" X 14" PIZZA

Ingredients
- 2½ cups (338g) **bread flour**
- 1 cup (237mL) **bottled water, warmed to 100°F (38°C)**
- 2 teaspoons (6g) **instant yeast**
- 1½ teaspoons (9g) **table salt**

1 In the work bowl of your stand mixer, add in the flour, water, yeast, and salt in that order.

2 Using the hook attachment, work for 5 minutes on low speed or until combined. The dough will be sticky.

3 Let the dough rest for 10 minutes as-is, then work it again for another 5 minutes on low speed.

4 Form the dough into a ball and move it to a large, greased bowl. Cover it and let it rise for 3–4 hours, punching it down once. The goal is for the dough to double in size before you're ready to cook.

DETROIT PIZZA SAUCE

MAKES ONE 10" X 14" PIZZA

Ingredients
- 2 tablespoons olive oil
- 2 cloves garlic, minced
- 2 cups crushed tomatoes
- ½ teaspoon onion powder
- 1 teaspoon brown sugar
- 1 teaspoon dried oregano
- 1 teaspoon dried basil
- ½ teaspoon red pepper flakes
- ½ teaspoon baking soda
- ¼ teaspoon kosher salt

1 Place a saucepot over medium heat and pour in the olive oil.

2 Once the oil is warm, add the garlic and cook for 1 minute, stirring the entire time.

3 Add in the tomatoes, then the onion powder, brown sugar, oregano, basil, red pepper flakes, baking soda, and salt. Cook on low heat for 20 minutes, stirring often.

4 Cool and set aside for future use.

KALAMAZOO-STYLE DOUGH (SEE PAGE 92)

MAKES ONE 14" PIZZA

Ingredients
- 2 cups (270g) bread flour
- ½ cup (135mL) bottled water, warmed to 100°F (38°C)
- 3 tablespoons (45mL) lager
- 1 teaspoon (4g) sugar
- 1 teaspoon (3g) instant yeast
- ¾ teaspoon (4g) table salt
- 3 tablespoons (42g) olive oil

1 In the work bowl of your stand mixer, gently combine the water, lager, sugar, yeast, and 1 cup of the flour. Let stand for 3 minutes.

2 Following the rest period, begin to mix using the hook attachment on low. Gently pour in the remaining flour, salt, and oil. Mix for 5 minutes on medium-low speed (scraping the bowl as needed to keep the dough in the bowl).

3 Transfer the dough to a large, greased bowl. Let it rise on the counter for 4 hours, punching it down once.

Gluten-Free Alternative

Gluten-free? Try making any of the Detroit pizzas with one batch of the gluten-free classic pan dough on page 71. Use either a 12" cast-iron pan or a 9" x 13" metal pan and use only 1 cup of sauce. Follow the instructions in the Detroit cheese pizza recipe on page 88.

Detroit Cheese Pizza

We begin our Detroit pizza journey with a classic cheese pie, but don't take the absence of toppings to mean that this is a simple pizza. The complex cheese, rich cooked sauce, and the frico around the rim make even a "plain" cheese Detroit pizza wildly interesting!

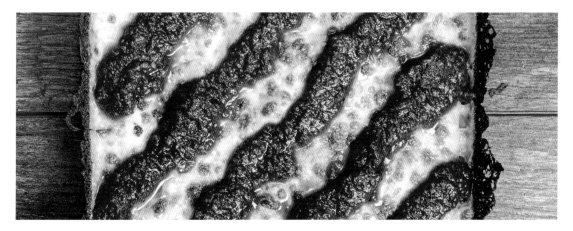

Inspiration: The texture on "The Frico King" Jim Henry's crust with the cheese frico against the saucy top and chewy, cheesy center is about as perfect as a pie can be.

Ingredients
- Detroit pizza dough, see page 86
- Detroit pizza sauce, see page 87
- 8 ounces Monterey Jack cheese, cubed
- 4 ounces provolone cheese, cubed
- 3 tablespoons grated Parmesan

Equipment
- 2 tablespoons corn oil
- 10" x 14" Detroit pizza pan or 9" x 13" metal pan

1 Prepare the dough and sauce.

2 Once the dough has risen, pour the corn oil into the pan. Swirl the oil around, then use a clean cloth to grease the corners of the pan.

3 Place the dough into the pan and gently press it into the bottom and corners. Once the dough has been formed, cover it and let it rise for another 30 minutes.

4 Preheat the oven to 475°F (245°C). Place a rack on the lowest slot of the oven.

5 Top the pizza with the cheese cubes (be sure to push them out to the sides), then the Parmesan. Dollop on the sauce in rows (one big spoonful every few inches). Bake on the lowest rack for 14–18 minutes or until the cheese is very dark brown.

6 Remove the cooked pizza from the oven and immediately free the pizza from the sides of the pan with a butter knife or spatula. Let cool for 5 minutes, transfer to a cutting board, cut into squares, serve, and enjoy!

Pepperoni and Frico Detroit

Detroit-style pizzas crave pepperoni. The chewy texture, subtle spiciness, and extreme savory notes play with these specific cheeses and sauce perfectly. By "hiding" some of the pepperoni under the cheese, we create a contrast of textures—the protected layer remains chewy while the top layer becomes crisp. Note the use of cornstarch, a trick borrowed from the amazing lattice structure formed when making potstickers. It promotes the tall cheese frico.

Inspiration: The master behind this pizza, Jim Henry, is a Detroit pizza legend. Look at that cheese frico!

Ingredients

- Detroit pizza dough, see page 86
- Detroit pizza sauce, see page 87
- 2 ounces mozzarella, shredded
- 1 tablespoon cornstarch
- 3 tablespoons grated Parmesan
- 5 ounces pepperoni, thickly hand-cut
- 8 ounces mozzarella, cubed
- 5 ounces sharp cheddar, cubed
- 10 basil leaves

Equipment

- 2 tablespoons corn oil
- 10" x 14" Detroit pizza pan or 9" x 13" metal pan

1 Prepare the dough and sauce.

2 Once the dough has risen, pour the corn oil into the pan. Swirl the oil around, then use a clean cloth to grease the corners of the pan.

3 Place the dough into the pan and gently press it into the bottom and corners. Once the dough has been formed, cover it and let it rise for another 30 minutes.

4 Preheat the oven to 475°F (245°C). Place a rack on the lowest slot of the oven.

5 Toss the shredded mozzarella with the cornstarch and half of the Parmesan.

6 Once the dough has rested within the pan, top it with two-thirds of the pepperoni, the cheese cubes, and the remaining pepperoni. Gently press the shredded cheese mixture into the sides of the pan, as high as you can go without protruding over the top. Dollop on the sauce in rows (one big spoonful every few inches).

7 Bake on the lowest rack for 14–18 minutes or until the cheese is very dark brown. Take extra care when removing the pizza from the pan so as to not shatter the cheese frico. It is most stable right out of the oven, so work fast! Once removed from the pan, garnish with the basil and serve.

Reuben Detroit

There are many amazing Detroit-style pizzerias, but there is one in particular that I feel rides the line between the classic heart of the Detroit and the culinary options this specific pizza is perfect for. Pie Sci Pizza in Detroit, Michigan, is a trendy pizza joint serving up creative pies in basic, counter-service digs. I appreciate that they cater to lots of dietary needs including vegan, vegetarian, and gluten free, which is not the easiest to nail with such a specific style of pizza. My favorite slice of theirs is a take on the classic Reuben called the Kraut at the Devil. It's so wonderfully rich that it will live in your mind rent-free for months. The brick cheese is a perfect foil for the salty and savory corned beef and the tangy sauerkraut. This is not a pie for the faint of heart, but it is the one the hooked me on Pie Sci and their wizardry. Let's be inspired by their idea and create a Reuben Detroit mashup ourselves.

Ingredients

- Detroit pizza dough, see page 86
- 6 ounces corned beef, chipped
- 4 ounces Swiss cheese, sliced
- 8 ounces Monterey Jack cheese, cubed
- ⅔ cup sauerkraut
- ½ cup thousand island dressing

Equipment

- 2 tablespoons corn oil
- 10" x 14" Detroit pizza pan or 9" x 13" metal pan

1 Prepare the dough.

2 Once the dough has risen, pour the corn oil into the pan. Swirl the oil around, then use a clean cloth to grease the corners of the pan.

3 Place the dough into the pan and gently press it into the bottom and corners. Once the dough has been formed, cover it and let it rise for another 30 minutes.

4 Preheat the oven to 475°F (245°C). Place a rack on the lowest slot of the oven.

5 Once the dough has rested within the pan, top it in this order: half the corned beef, the Swiss cheese, the Monterey Jack cheese, and finally the remaining corned beef.

6 Bake on the lowest rack for 14–18 minutes or until the cheese is very dark brown. Top with sauerkraut and a drizzle of thousand island dressing (and please do not tell your cardiologist what we just did).

Inspiration: Pie Sci's Reuben is just about the best bite of food one could ever imagine. The fermented kraut pulls out flavors from the crust, and the corned beef and dressing add the salty, savory, and sweet notes of the classic sandwich.

Kalamazoo-Style Pizza

I hear your internal monologue now: what the heck is Kalamazoo-style pizza? First, a geography lesson. Kalamazoo, Michigan (where I happen to live) is about halfway between Chicago and Detroit, and the culture here is influenced by both cities. Additionally, Kalamazoo is an incredible beer town, with many craft breweries in the area. So, in honor of both the region and culture here, I created this pizza to honor the city.

   Getting into the recipe, a Kalamazoo-style pizza is part Chicago tavern (see page 176) and part Detroit. First, the dough is closer to the Chicago tavern-style pizza, though I spike this recipe with a bit of beer. Next, the sauce is sweeter like a pub style, with the use of the tomato paste. As for the eastern inspiration of this pie, the cheese is a mix akin to brick cheese we use for traditional Detroits. Finally, the ingredients are layered so that the sauce is above the cheese, creating that signature Detroit look. In total, this pizza is a perfect homage to Kalamazoo, and one of the tastiest pies I have ever made.

Ingredients

- Kalamazoo-style dough, see page 87
- 2 tablespoons olive oil
- 2 teaspoons tomato paste
- 1 cup crushed tomatoes
- 2 teaspoons Italian seasoning

- 6 ounces Monterey Jack cheese, cubed
- 4 ounces provolone cheese, cubed
- 3 tablespoons grated Parmesan
- 5 ounces pepperoni, thickly hand-cut

Equipment

- Olive oil for greasing
- 14" round, lipped pizza pan

Cutting a pizza into 2" squares is called the "party cut"!

1 Sometime before pizza day, combine the olive oil, tomato paste, crushed tomatoes, a pinch of salt, and Italian seasoning into small saucepot. Bring it to just a simmer, whisking in the tomato paste, and cook on low for 15 minutes. Chill until ready to use.

2 Prepare the dough. Once the dough is finished with the bench proof, preheat the oven to 450°F (235°C).

3 Roll the dough into a 14" circle, grease the pizza pan, then lay the dough into the pan without adding a lip.

4 Top the pizza with the cheese cubes (be sure to push them out to the sides). Dollop on the sauce in rows (one big spoonful every few inches). Finish with the pepperoni.

5 Bake the pizza for 15–17 minutes or until very brown on all sides (I have found that the middle or lower rack is best).

6 Once the pizza is cooked, remove it from the oven and immediately free it from the pan with a butter knife. Garnish with the Parmesan, then let it cool for 2 minutes.

7 Transfer the pizza to a cutting board using two spatulas and cut into 2" squares. Serve and enjoy!

This is an interesting hybrid pie. Note the crisp cheese crust, relative thinness, and the sauce on top. The result is a pizza that is in between a pan, a thin, and a Sicilian, taking the best aspects of each.

Kalamazoo

MI

New England Greek

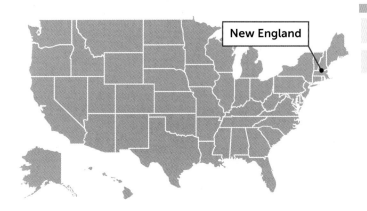

New England

NEW ENGLAND GREEK PIZZA DOUGH

MAKES ONE 14" PIZZA

Ingredients
- **3 cups (400g) bread flour**
- **1 cup plus a splash (260mL) warm water**
- **1½ teaspoons (4.5g) instant yeast**
- **1 teaspoon (6g) table salt**
- **2 tablespoons (28g) olive oil**

New England Greek pizza is a cross between a hand-tossed Manhattan and a fast-food pan pizza . . . in the absolute best way. This pizza is named not for classic Greek toppings like feta or olives, but rather for the fact that the originating pizza shops are usually owned by or have been established by Greek immigrants. Most Greek pizza joints have "House of Pizza" (or HoP) in the name. It's a trademark of the area (as of writing, there are close to 300 pizzerias with "House of Pizza" somewhere in the business name).

1 In your stand mixer or large bowl, gently combine the water, sugar, yeast, and 1 cup of the flour. Let stand for 5 minutes.

2 Following the rest period, begin to mix using the hook attachment on low. Gently pour in the remaining flour, salt, and oil. Mix for 8 minutes on medium-low speed (scraping the bowl as needed to keep the dough in the bowl).

3 Transfer the dough to a large, greased bowl. Let it rise on the counter for 2 hours, then in the fridge overnight.

4 Remove the dough from the fridge 2–3 hours before cooking.

NEW ENGLAND GREEK PIZZA SAUCE

MAKES ONE 10" X 14" PIZZA

Ingredients

- 2 tablespoons olive oil
- 1 tablespoon tomato paste
- 3 cloves garlic, minced
- 1½ cups crushed tomatoes
- 1 teaspoon oregano
- 1 pinch red pepper flakes

1 Sometime before pizza day, combine the olive oil, tomato paste, garlic, and a pinch of salt in a small saucepot.

2 Cook on low, stirring constantly, for 5 minutes. Add in the crushed tomatoes, oregano, and red pepper flakes and bring to just a simmer, whisking to melt in the tomato paste.

3 Simmer, covered, on low for 30 minutes or until it's reduced by a third, then chill it until you're ready to cook.

LARD PIZZA DOUGH

MAKES ONE 14" PIZZA

Ingredients

- 3 cups (400g) bread flour
- 1 cup plus a splash (260mL) warm water
- 1½ teaspoons (4.5g) instant yeast
- 1 teaspoon (4g) sugar
- 1 teaspoon (6g) table salt
- 3 tablespoons (42g) lard, chilled

1 In your stand mixer or large bowl, gently combine the water, sugar, yeast, and 1 cup of the flour. Let stand for 5 minutes.

2 Following the rest period, begin to mix using the hook attachment on low. Gently pour in the remaining flour, salt, and lard. Mix for 8 minutes on medium-low speed.

3 Transfer the dough to a large, greased bowl. Let it rise on the counter for 4 hours, then in the fridge overnight.

4 Move the dough directly from the fridge to the floured work surface just before cooking.

Gluten-Free Alternative

Gluten-free? Try making any of the New England Greek pizzas with one batch of the gluten-free classic pan dough on page 71 to make one 12" pizza. Reduce the sauce to ½ cup, and use only 4 ounces of mozzarella, 3 ounces of provolone, and 3 ounces of white cheddar, all grated. Follow the instructions in the GF pan recipe on page 75.

Cheese Greek Pizza

My first experience with a HoP was in Lancaster, New Hampshire, aptly named Lancaster House of Pizza. A family-owned restaurant, this pizzeria is a no-nonsense spot serving a really nice Greek pie. Lower on the greasiness than other HoPs, the pizzas here are perhaps a little closer to a hand-tossed pie, which is a plus in my book. To be completely transparent, this was probably the most difficult pizza to get just right. Thanks to several test pizzas and a little research, I discovered that the key lies in the use of shortening in the pizza pan and the combination of cheeses used. The result is a remarkably crisp pizza that is deliciously heavy and rich, with a complex cheese layer that you'll dream about later.

■ **Inspiration:**
A straightforward, classic LHOP pizza, featuring just the right amount of greasiness for maximum enjoyment.

A hair lighter than a traditional LHOP, but still maintaining that dense, slick flavor with the sweet sauce and chewy crust.

Ingredients
- New England Greek pizza dough, see page 94
- New England Greek pizza sauce, see page 95
- 4 tablespoons shortening or butter
- 6 ounces mozzarella, grated
- 4 ounces provolone, grated
- 4 ounces white cheddar, grated
- 2 tablespoons Parmesan

Equipment
- Butter or shortening, for the pan
- 14" round, lipped pizza pan

1 Sometime before pizza day, prepare the sauce.

2 Remove the dough from the fridge 2–3 hours before cooking. Preheat the oven to 475°F (245°C) and move a rack to the lower third of the oven.

3 Grease the pan liberally with the shortening or butter. Move the dough onto a floured surface and form it into a 12"–14" circle. Move the dough into the pan, pressing it into the sides to form the slightest of lips.

4 Following the bench proof, top the pizza with the sauce and the mozzarella, provolone, white cheddar, and Parmesan.

5 Bake the pizza for 16–20 minutes or until it's deeply golden. Once cooked, remove it from the pan, cut it into slices, and devour.

"Greek" Greek Pizza

Hey, I get it, you heard Greek pizza, and you want Greek toppings. Why not have both? I enjoy this one for many reasons, but most of all for the heavy oregano, both in the sauce and in the finish.

Tomatoes, olives, and four different cheeses make this a "Greek" Greek Pizza.

■ **Inspiration:**
A Greek pizza by LHoP's Greek pizza maker, where the chewy crust and copious amounts of cheese stand up to the classic Greek salad veggies.

Ingredients

- New England Greek pizza dough, see page 94
- New England Greek pizza sauce, see page 95
- ¼ cup cooked, drained, and chopped spinach
- 8 ounces mozzarella, grated
- 3 ounces provolone, grated
- 3 ounces feta cheese, crumbled
- 2 tablespoons Parmesan
- 2 tablespoons black olives, sliced
- ½ Roma tomato, diced
- 2 garlic cloves, minced
- 2 teaspoons dried oregano

Equipment

- Butter or shortening, for the pan
- 14" round, lipped pizza pan

1 Sometime before pizza day, prepare the sauce.

2 Remove the dough from the fridge 2–3 hours before cooking. Preheat the oven to 475°F (245°C) and move a rack to the lower third of the oven.

3 Grease the pan liberally with the shortening or butter. Move the dough onto a floured surface and form it into a 12"–14" circle. Move the dough into the pan, pressing it into the sides to form the slightest of lips.

4 Following the bench proof, top the pizza with the sauce, spinach, cheeses, olives, tomatoes, and garlic.

5 Bake the pizza for 16–20 minutes or until it's deeply golden. Once cooked, garnish with the dried oregano and serve.

Lard Pan Pizza

In testing the Greek pizza, I accidentally created one of the best pan pizzas on the planet. This recipe has a few changeups. First, we will be using lard instead of oil in the dough (which is historically accurate to some versions of this pizza). You could also use shortening. Second, we will be pushing the cheese right out to the edge, allowing it to caramelize with the fat in the dough. The result is a cheese crust beyond your wildest dreams.

Ingredients
- Lard pizza dough, see page 95
- New England Greek pizza sauce, see page 95
- 6 ounces mozzarella, grated
- 3 ounces provolone, grated
- 3 ounces white cheddar, grated
- 2 tablespoons Parmesan

Equipment
- 14" round, lipped pizza pan

1 Sometime before pizza day, prepare the sauce.

2 Preheat the oven to 475°F (245°C) and move a rack to the lower third of the oven.

3 Move the dough directly from the fridge onto a floured surface and form it into a 12"–14" circle. Move the dough into the pan, pressing it into the sides to form the slightest of lips, then let it rise for another 30 minutes. **Note:** There is no need to grease the pan here, as the fat in the dough will do the job.

4 Following the bench proof, top the pizza with the sauce and the mozzarella, provolone, and white cheddar, pushing the cheese right out to the pan. Finish with the Parmesan.

5 Bake the pizza for 14–18 minutes or until it's deeply golden and charred around the edges. Once cooked, use a butter knife to free the pizza from the sides of the pan. Transfer it to a cutting board and cut it into thick slices.

> If you want to include other toppings, add them on top of the grated cheeses before you add the Parmesan.

Lard might seem like an odd ingredient choice, but it brings out a fullness in the cheesy flavor that's unbeatable.

Colorado Mountain

Colorado

MAKES ONE 14" PIZZA

Ingredients
- 1½ cups (200g) **bread flour**
- 1¼ cups (162g) **whole wheat flour**
- 1 cup (237mL) **water**
- 2 tablespoons (42g) **honey**
- 1 tablespoon (9g) **instant yeast**
- 1 teaspoon (6g) **salt**
- 2 tablespoons (28g) **olive oil**

This pizza, my friends, is going to make it into your regular rotation. The Colorado mountain–style pizza is as bold and massive as the Rocky Mountains, featuring a big flavorful crust (thanks to the use of whole wheat flour and honey). This pie demands a boulder of toppings and is both forgiving and rewarding to make at home. Colorado mountain pizza is often sold by the pound, not the slice, and is always served with honey to accompany the crust.

1 In your stand mixer or a large bowl, combine the water, honey, and yeast. Let stand for 3 minutes.

2 Following the rest period, begin to mix using the hook attachment on low. Pour in the flours, salt, and oil. Mix for 5 minutes on low speed. This dough will be tackier than most.

3 Remove from the mixer and form the dough into a ball, then place it back into the work bowl.

4 Let the dough rise for 4–6 hours, punching it down once.

COLORADO MOUNTAIN SAUCE

Ingredients

- 2 tablespoons olive oil
- 1 cup crushed tomatoes
- 1 tablespoon tomato paste
- 3 cloves garlic, minced
- 1 pinch red pepper flakes
- 1 teaspoon Italian seasoning

1 Combine the olive oil, crushed tomatoes, tomato paste, garlic, a pinch of salt, red pepper flakes, and Italian seasoning in a small saucepot.

2 Bring to just a simmer and cook for 5 minutes to combine all the ingredients. Set aside and cool until you're ready to cook.

THINNED-DOWN COLORADO MOUNTAIN DOUGH

MAKES ONE 14" PIZZA

Ingredients

- ¾ cup (100g) bread flour
- ⅔ cup (86g) whole wheat flour
- ½ cup plus a splash (118mL) bottled water
- 1 tablespoon (21g) honey
- 1 tablespoon (9g) instant yeast
- ½ teaspoon (3g) salt
- 1 tablespoon (14g) olive oil

1 In your stand mixer or a large bowl, combine the water, honey, and yeast. Let stand for 3 minutes.

2 Following the rest period, begin to mix using the hook attachment on low. Pour in the flours, salt, and oil. Mix for 5 minutes on low speed. This dough will be tackier than most.

3 Remove from the mixer and form the dough into a ball, then place it back into the work bowl.

4 Let the dough rise for 4–6 hours, punching it down once.

Colorado Mountain Pie

You cannot talk about Colorado mountain pizza without also mentioning Beau Jo's, an institution around Colorado. With a decades-long history, they have singlehandedly created and popularized mountain pizza. With the signature hand-rolled edge and toppings galore, this is a must-have when in Colorado. If you don't have a 14" lipped pizza pan, get one. Until then, don't be afraid to improvise and use a large cake pan, paella pan, or whatever you have that is big enough! Take your time with the braid on this one, which really helps build the volume of the crust, holding in the toppings nicely.

Ingredients
- Colorado mountain dough, see page 100
- Colorado mountain sauce, see page 101
- 14 ounces mozzarella cheese, shredded
- 3 ounces pepperoni, sliced
- Honey for drizzling
- ¼ cup basil leaves, torn

Equipment
- Oil or nonstick spray, for the pan
- 14" round, lipped pizza pan

1 Prepare the dough and sauce.

2 Preheat the oven to 450°F (235°C) and grease the pan with oil or nonstick spray.

3 Roll the dough into a flat 16" circle and move it into the pan, leaving a 1" overhang. Dock the dough (poke holes into it to let steam release during baking) with a fork.

4 Make small slits in the overhanging dough every few inches. Roll the dough back in toward the pie to form a crimped crust lip. **Note:** There's no need for perfection; you just want to create some volume with your roll. If the braiding is too difficult, simply roll the excess onto itself.

5 Top the pizza with the sauce, being careful to preserve the lip. Add the cheese and pepperoni.

6 Bake the pizza for 18–22 minutes or until it's golden. Once cooked, drizzle the pizza with honey and finish with the torn basil.

If the braid is a bit challenging, let it bench rise after rolling for 15 minutes to help everything form back together.

Inspiration:
Look at the volume Beau Jo's achieves on their crust, which is light and nutty from the wheat flour.

Colorado Supreme Pizza

My favorite combination of toppings at Beau Jo's is the Hamburger. A supremely supreme pizza, this one is worth the flight alone. You can also add an equal part of sweet Italian sausage, if you really want to go "full send" (and you definitely do).

Inspiration: Beau Jo's isn't afraid of the toppings, which is great on a pizza like this one. The thick, hearty crust can easily support all of the meats, cheeses, and veggies.

Ingredients

- Colorado mountain dough, see page 100
- Colorado mountain sauce, see page 101
- 14 ounces mozzarella cheese, shredded
- 4 ounces cooked ground beef
- ¼ cup diced green peppers
- ¼ cup mushrooms, sliced and sautéed
- ¼ cup diced red onion
- 2 tablespoons grated Parmesan
- 3 ounces pepperoni, sliced
- Honey for drizzling

Equipment

- Oil or nonstick spray, for the pan
- 14" round, lipped pizza pan

1 Prepare the dough and sauce.

2 Preheat the oven to 450°F (235°C) and grease the pan with oil or nonstick spray.

3 Roll the dough into a flat 16" circle and move it into the pan, leaving a 1" overhang. Dock the dough (poke holes into it to let steam release during baking) with a fork.

4 Make small slits in the overhanging dough every few inches. Roll the dough back in toward the pie to form a crimped crust lip. **Note:** There's no need for perfection; you just want to create some volume with your roll. If the braiding is too difficult, simply roll the excess onto itself.

5 Top the pizza with the sauce, mozzarella, ground beef, peppers, mushrooms, onion, Parmesan, and pepperoni.

6 Bake the pizza for 18–22 minutes or until it's golden. Once cooked, drizzle the pizza with honey.

Colorado Hot Honey Pie

Another signature of pies in and around Colorado is the post-cook addition of hot honey, which is as ubiquitous as a pepper shaker in a New York pizza shop. We will lean into this trend with a pie of our own, featuring hot honey, spicy pepperoni, and enough ricotta to cool everything down. Also note that the dough will be much thinner here—in addition to the large mountain pies, most Colorado spots feature a thinned-down version that is perfect for this pie.

Ricotta dollops on top add a contrast of cool relief to the spicy hot honey and red pepper flakes.

Ingredients

- Thinned-down Colorado mountain dough, see page 101
- Colorado mountain sauce, see page 101
- 8 ounces mozzarella cheese, grated
- 3 ounces pepperoni, sliced
- 1 cup whipped ricotta
- 3 tablespoons hot honey

Equipment

- Oil or nonstick spray, for the pan
- 14" round, lipped pizza pan

1 Prepare the dough and sauce.

2 Preheat the oven to 450°F (235°C) and grease the pan with oil or nonstick spray.

3 Stretch the dough into a 12"–14" circle on the pizza pan, leaving a slight lip.

4 Top the pizza with the sauce, mozzarella, and pepperoni.

5 Bake the pizza for 12–14 minutes or until very bubbly and brown. Let it cool slightly, then top with swirls of the hot honey and dollops of the ricotta.

Cuban

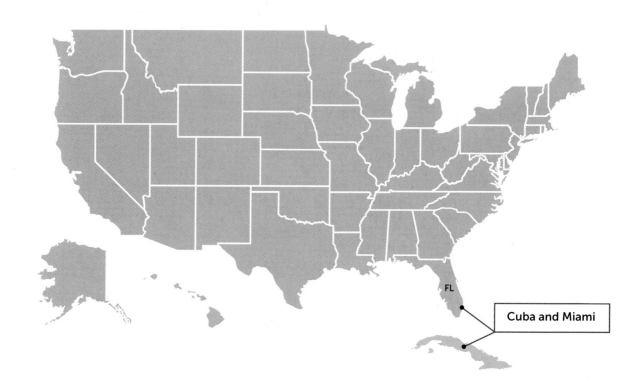

FL

Cuba and Miami

When you hear "Cuban-style pizza," don't immediately think of the ham, pickles, and mustard of a Cuban sandwich. Instead, think of a wonderful pan pizza with Cuban flair: The sauce, extremely tangy with spices; the cheese, strong and sharp, pushed right out to the edge; and toppings as wild as you can imagine. (Cooked chorizo and pickled onions are a popular combo.) Yes, Miami's Cuban-style pizza is a hidden gem of a pie that relies on a secret ingredient, Gouda cheese. This Gouda (like in the Cuban sandwich) offers a buttery depth to the entire pie, which pairs with the thickness of the pizza perfectly. The pizza then eats somewhere between a Detroit and a classic pan, but might actually be better than either.

CUBAN PIZZA DOUGH

MAKES ONE 12" PIZZA

Ingredients

- 2⅓ cups (315g) all-purpose flour
- ¾ cup plus a splash (192mL) water, warmed to 110°F (45°C)
- ½ tablespoon (2g) sugar
- 3 tablespoons (42g) olive oil
- 2 teaspoons (6g) instant yeast
- 1 teaspoon (6g) table salt

1 In your stand mixer or a large bowl, combine the water, sugar, oil, flour, yeast, and salt in that order. Gently mix on medium for 5 minutes.

2 Transfer the dough to a large bowl sprayed with nonstick spray and let the dough rise on the counter for 8 hours, punching it down every other hour.

CUBAN PIZZA SAUCE

MAKES ONE 12" PIZZA

Ingredients

- 3 tablespoons olive oil
- ¼ cup minced green pepper
- ¼ onion, minced
- 2 cloves garlic, minced
- 1 cup crushed tomatoes
- ½ teaspoon kosher salt
- 1 tablespoon sugar
- 1 teaspoon paprika
- 1 teaspoon dried oregano
- Lemon juice, to taste

1 In a small saucepan over medium heat, add the olive oil and sauté the green pepper, onion, and garlic until softened, 5–6 minutes.

2 Add the crushed tomatoes, kosher salt, sugar, paprika, and oregano and stir well. Simmer for 5–10 minutes until the sauce is just a little thicker and slightly reduced.

3 Finish with lemon juice and keep cool until ready to cook.

Gluten-Free Alternative

Gluten-free? Try making any of the Cuban pizzas with one batch of the gluten-free classic pan dough on page 71. Reduce the sauce to ½ cup, and follow the instructions in the GF pan recipe on page 75.

Cuban-Style Pizza

So how did pizza mash up with Cuban food, anyway? Well, according to Elizabeth Borges, master pizza maker in the Miami area, the history dates back the to the 1930s:

> Pizza arrived in Cuba in the 1930s along with many Italians who came to the island to build churches, houses, [etc.] . . . and with them they brought the pizza recipe and that is how the Cuban recipes merged with the Italian ones and that is how the Cuban pizza was born. Gradually, Cubans modified them in their own way. It is customary to bake them in frying pans and we eat the pizzas folded in half.

Just like many other styles of pizza, we see a gentle integration into the local culture. Let's honor this culinary mashup with a pie of our own, shall we?

Ingredients
- Cuban pizza dough, see page 107
- Cuban pizza sauce, see page 107
- 6 ounces Gouda, grated
- 4 ounces mozzarella, grated

Equipment
- 12" pizza pan or cast-iron skillet

1 Prepare the dough and sauce.

2 Preheat the oven to 475°F (245°C).

3 Roll the dough into a 12" circle with no lip and place it on the pizza pan.

4 Top the pizza with the sauce and cheeses, running all the toppings out to the edge of the pizza.

5 Bake the pizza for 12–16 minutes or until bubbly.

The Gouda and mozzarella just melt wonderfully on this pie, making a buttery, creamy cheese blend that is unique to this style.

■ *Inspiration:*
Look at these
beauties from
Pa' Comer—each
has melty cheese
bordered by crunchy,
caramelized crust.
The range of Gouda
is such that it shines
both melted and
burnt along the rim.

Chorizo Cuban Pizza

One of my favorite pizza places on this planet, Pa' Comer, is run by pizza legend Elizabeth Borges. Pa' is an informal abbreviation of the Spanish word *para* (meaning "for"), which is very common slang in Cuba—Pa' Comer translates to "for eating," something I do plenty of when I stop by! Chef Elizabeth has been making classic Cuban pies for over 10 years and was one of the first in the Miami area to do so. Let's honor one of her most famous creations, the chorizo pizza. Yes, we are only adding one ingredient to the basic Cuban-style pizza recipe on page 108, but repurposing the chorizo fat adds an incredible layer of flavor that creates a completely different pie.

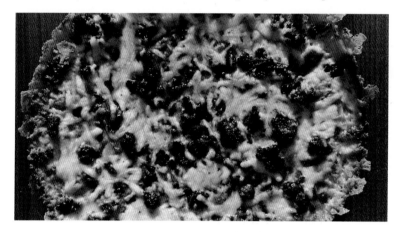

Christy Alia (see page 27) is a pizza master (and the maker and photographer of this particular pizza). The height on that cheese and the wonderful cook on the pie show true skill.

■ **Inspiration:** The authentic Cuban-American chorizo on Pa' Comer's pizza is worth a flight to Miami alone.

Ingredients
- Cuban pizza dough, see page 107
- Cuban pizza sauce, see page 107
- 6 ounces Gouda, grated
- 4 ounces mozzarella, grated
- 6 ounces fresh chorizo

Equipment
- 12" pizza pan or cast-iron skillet

1 Prepare the dough and sauce.

2 As the dough is rising, crumble the chorizo into a large saucepan over medium heat and cook for 6–8 minutes. Use a slotted spoon to remove the cooked meat, and reserve the rendered fat separately.

3 Preheat the oven to 475°F (245°C). Brush the pan with the rendered chorizo fat.

4 Roll the dough into a 12" circle with no lip and place it on the pizza pan.

5 Top the pizza with the sauce, one-third of the chorizo, the cheeses, and then the remaining chorizo.

6 Bake the pizza for 12–16 minutes or until brown and crisp.

Calzones and More

This section celebrates all forms of rolled, filled, and stuffed pizza. We will start with the classic Calzone, which is a favorite for good reason and needs no description. Take a pizza, fold it in half, seal it, bake it, and eat it. Many calzone recipes use a normal Neapolitan pizza dough, but I find that a lower-hydration dough is easier to work with and produces a better crisp exterior and non-soggy interior. Go wild with this one, because it cooks so wonderfully at home. Note the cubed cheese, which will melt just a hair slower, protecting against cheese eruptions during baking.

CALZONE DOUGH

MAKES TWO CALZONES, ONE STROMBOLI, TWO SCACCIATA, OR TWELVE ROLLS

Ingredients

- 2 cups (270g) bread flour
- ⅔ cup (158mL) water, warmed to 100–110°F (38–45°C)
- 1 tablespoon (12g) sugar
- 2 teaspoons (6g) instant yeast
- ¾ teaspoon (4.5g) table salt
- 2 tablespoons (28g) extra-virgin olive oil, plus more for greasing

1 In your stand mixer or a large bowl, gently combine the water, sugar, yeast, and 1 cup of flour. Let stand for 5 minutes.

2 Following the rest period, mix on low using the hook attachment or your hands. Gently pour in the remaining flour, salt, and oil. Mix for 6 minutes on medium-low speed.

3 Form the dough into a ball and transfer it to a large, greased bowl. Let the dough rise for 2–4 hours.

BREADSTICK DOUGH

MAKES EIGHT LARGE BREADSTICKS

Ingredients

- 2 cups (270g) bread flour
- ⅔ cup (158mL) water, warmed to 100–110°F (38–45°C)
- 1 tablespoon (12g) sugar
- ¾ teaspoon (4.5g) table salt
- 2 teaspoons (6g) instant yeast
- 2 tablespoons (28g) extra-virgin olive oil

1 In a large mixing bowl, combine the flour, sugar, salt, and yeast. Add the oil, then gradually add the water while mixing until a dough forms.

2 Transfer the dough to a floured surface and knead for 5–7 minutes until it becomes smooth and elastic.

3 Place the dough in a lightly oiled bowl, cover it with a damp cloth, and let it rise in a warm place for 1–2 hours or until it doubles in size.

Pepperoni and Cheese Calzone

Magic happens when you fold dough over cheese and other pizza toppings and bake it. The fillings meld nicely, letting their flavors intermingle in the best way. The use of the three cheeses here along with pepperoni makes for a classic pizza flavor that shines against the crisp calzone crust.

More than just a folded pizza, the calzone's shape allows for the fillings to intermingle when cooking. The pepperoni grease fries the cheese, adding a bit of texture as well as a deeper pepperoni flavor throughout.

Ingredients

- Calzone dough, see page 111
- 4 ounces provolone cheese, cubed
- 4 ounces mozzarella, cubed
- 4 ounces pepperoni, divided
- ¼ cup grated Parmesan
- Tomato sauce for dipping (try your favorite recipe from this book)

Equipment

- 14" pizza pan

1 Prepare the dough.

2 Preheat the oven to 450°F (235°C). Divide the dough in half, then move the two halves onto a floured surface. Form each into a 12" circle.

3 Fill each dough circle with half of the cubed cheeses, Parmesan, and pepperoni, leaving a 1" lip around the edge.

4 Fold each circle in half and crease the edges to seal. Cut three small openings in the top of each calzone.

5 Bake on the pan for 12–15 minutes or until golden. Transfer to a cutting board, cut into three slices, and enjoy.

Classic Stromboli

A calzone is dough that's folded in half over the toppings and sealed, while a stromboli is like an Italian cinnamon roll—it's a rectangle of dough that's filled, rolled, and baked. While the ingredients are essentially the same, thanks to the technique this is an entirely new dish. Some recipes call for the entire roll to be baked (as in this one), while others slice, then bake. Personally, I like having the cheese and ingredients meld mid-bake, but the choice is yours.

Beyond a rolled pizza, the stromboli is the ultimate picnic lunch, make-ahead buffet dish, or light dinner treat.

Ingredients

- Calzone dough, see page 111
- 4 ounces provolone cheese, shredded
- 4 ounces mozzarella, sliced
- 4 ounces ham, sliced
- ¼ cup grated Parmesan, divided
- Olive oil for topping
- Tomato sauce for dipping

Equipment

- 18" x 13" baking sheet

When you're rolling out the dough, use a bit of flour as needed to prevent the dough from sticking.

1 Prepare the dough.

2 Preheat the oven to 375°F (190°C).

3 Once the dough has risen, roll it out as close as you can get it to the size of the baking sheet.

4 Align the wide edge with the counter's edge. Sprinkle on half the Parmesan, then layer on the provolone, mozzarella, and ham, being sure to leave a 1" border around the edge.

5 Once the fillings are in, sprinkle on the remaining Parmesan, then roll everything into a log, being sure to fold in the ends as you roll (like a massive burrito).

6 Once rolled, press the seam to seal. Grease the baking sheet, then place the stromboli seam-down on the sheet. Brush the top with olive oil and make a few diagonal slits in the top.

7 Bake for 25–30 minutes or until golden. Slice thick and serve warm with the sauce on the side.

Beef Roll

In North-Central Illinois, where I worked in my 20s, local pizzerias would make this wonderful food called simply a "beef roll." An amalgamation of a stuffed Chicago pizza and an Italian beef, these rolls looked a bit like a pizza but tasted more like a sandwich. I argue that there is no better snack while huddled over a computer at 2 a.m. My favorite beef roll is from Enzo's Pizza in Villa Park, Illinois, where they lean into the beauty of this calzone variant; this recipe is a tribute to their masterpiece. If you have the means, pair this with some Chicago giardiniera, roasted peppers, or nacho cheese sauce. Think of this one for gameday hosting, as it is a winner for a crowd.

Chicagoland

Inspiration: Enzo's legendary beef roll is the best lunch, dinner, or 2 a.m. snack you could dream of—beef, cheese, and a wonderful bready bite. Note the cheese pull and color on the crust from the garlic powder, which adds a distinct flavor to the roll.

Ingredients

- Calzone dough, see page 111
- 10 ounces mozzarella cheese, shredded
- 10 ounces roast beef (Chicago Italian beef is best)
- 1 tablespoon butter, melted
- ½ teaspoon garlic powder
- 4 cups beef broth
- 1 tablespoon dried oregano

Equipment

- 18" x 13" baking sheet

> When you're rolling out the dough, use a bit of flour as needed to prevent the dough from sticking.

1 Prepare the dough.

2 Preheat the oven to 425°F (220°C).

3 Once the dough has risen, roll it out as close as you can get it to the size of the baking sheet.

4 Align the wide edge with the counter's edge. Evenly distribute the mozzarella and beef, being sure to leave a 1" border around the edge.

5 Once the fillings are in, roll the dough into itself twice, bringing the far edge halfway in and the near edge in to meet it to create a 5" x 13" log.

6 Brush the top of the roll with butter and sprinkle on the garlic powder. Grease the baking sheet, then place the roll on top. Bake for 20–22 minutes.

7 As the roll cooks, bring the broth to a simmer in a saucepot, spiking it with the oregano.

8 Once the roll is baked, let it cool for 5 minutes, then cut it into manageable portions (I like to cut it lengthwise, then into strips). Serve it with the seasoned broth for dipping.

Pepperoni Rolls

You can't go to a pizzeria in West Virginia without encountering a pepperoni roll. Somewhere between a stromboli and a calzone, these snacks are just as wonderful as they look and sound. Originally created as a lunch for coal miners on the go, feel free to experiment with the fillings—Gouda and ham make really wonderful picnic fare.

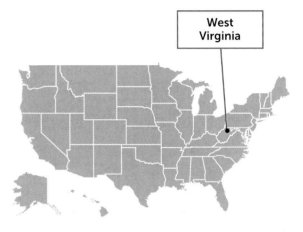

West Virginia

Pepperoni rolls are unrivaled for their convenience, taste, and ability to fill your belly up. The pepperoni fries the dough from the inside, making the middle of these delights spicy and lightly greasy.

Ingredients

- Calzone dough, see page 111
- 6 ounces pepperoni, sliced
- 10 ounces mozzarella cheese, shredded
- 2 ounces grated Parmesan
- ¼ cup chopped fresh parsley
- Olive oil for brushing

Equipment

- 13" x 18" baking pan

1 Prepare the dough.

2 Preheat the oven to 425°F (220°C).

3 Once the dough has risen, roll it out as close as you can get it to 12" x 18". Cut the dough in half lengthwise to make two 18" x 6" strips. Cut each long strip into six 3" x 6" rectangles (you should have twelve rectangles total).

4 Evenly distribute the pepperoni and mozzarella onto the dough rectangles, then roll each by taking the 6" end and folding it over onto and just under itself, making mini dough burritos.

5 Place the assembled rolls on the baking sheet, brush each with olive oil, and top them with the grated Parmesan cheese.

6 Bake for 12–14 minutes or until golden brown. Remove them from the oven, garnish with the parsley, and serve.

When you're rolling out the dough, use a bit of flour as needed to prevent the dough from sticking.

Scacciata

Scacciata is a traditional Sicilian stuffed flatbread. It is often filled with a savory mixture, and the dough is folded over to encase the filling. The filling can vary but commonly includes ingredients like ricotta cheese, mozzarella, Parmesan, and herbs. Think of this as a cousin to the common calzone, though perhaps more savory and cheesier.

Ingredients

- Calzone dough, see page 111
- 1½ cups ricotta cheese
- 1 cup mozzarella cheese, shredded
- ¼ cup grated Parmesan
- ¼ cup chopped fresh parsley
- 2 ounces prosciutto, sliced thin
- Olive oil for brushing

Equipment

- 14" Pizza Pan

1 Prepare the dough.

2 Preheat the oven to 425°F (220°C).

3 Once the dough has risen, roll it out as close as you can get it to the size of a 13" x 18" baking sheet. Cut the dough in half to make two 9" x 13" rectangles.

4 In a bowl, combine the ricotta, mozzarella, Parmesan, and parsley. Mix well.

5 Spread the cheese mixture evenly over one of the dough rectangles, leaving a border around the edge. Top with a few slices of prosciutto, then place the second dough rectangle on top and seal the edges.

6 Brush the top of the scacciata with olive oil, then place it on the pizza pan. Bake for 20–25 minutes or until golden brown. Allow it to cool for a few minutes before slicing.

> When you're rolling out the dough, use a bit of flour as needed to prevent the dough from sticking.

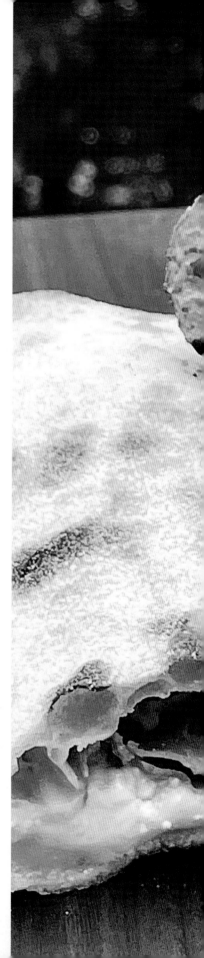

So light and crisp, with the subtle flavor from the ricotta shining through—this is more than a calzone. It eats almost like a puff pastry.

Sicily, Italy

Sausage Pizza Puffs

While our next offering has "pizza" in the name, admittedly this pizza puff strays a bit from traditional pies. That being said, these wonderful snacks are one of Chicago's best-kept secrets. A flat, fried pocket of pizza-type fillings like cheese and sausage, these little jewels have roots in the Middle East. The outside is somewhere between an egg roll and puff pastry, making it super crisp and inviting. Often served with marinara or mild sauce (a sweet-and-spicy Chicago condiment), pizza puffs are the ultimate after-school (or pub crawl) snack.

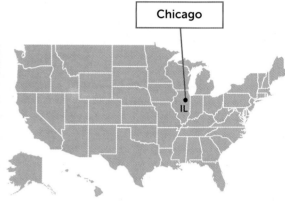

Chicago

A Chicagoland snack that is unrivaled, where the sausage and tomatoes make a sweet-and-savory classic flavor pairing.

Ingredients

- Four 12" flour tortillas
- 4 ounces Italian sausage, cooked and crumbled
- ½ cup tomato sauce (try your favorite recipe from this book)
- 6 ounces mozzarella cheese, shredded

Equipment

- 2 quarts neutral oil, for frying
- Large Dutch oven
- Large toothpicks

1 Heat the frying oil in a large Dutch oven to 350°F (175°C).

2 Fill the center of one tortilla with 1 ounce of the sausage, 1–2 tablespoons of sauce, and 1½ ounces of the cheese.

3 Imagine a square ½" in from the edge of the tortilla. Fold the side in along the edges of the imaginary square, then fold in the top and bottom. Use a toothpick or two to hold the puff in place.

4 Repeat steps 2 and 3 with the remaining tortillas and fillings.

5 Fry each pizza puff for 2–3 minutes. Remove them from the oil and set them aside on a draining rack. Serve warm.

Basic Breadsticks

Every pizza should be accompanied by a breadstick. I recommend making rectangular breadsticks, which are not only easier to form but cook much more evenly than the hand-rolled variant. If you want to freeform a breadstick, be sure to divide and carefully weigh the dough before rolling. These little breadsticks are a perfect treat that comes together in a snap.

Square breadsticks are not only easier to make, but they are also much more consistent when cooked. Freeform breadsticks are fun, but this is the way to go.

Ingredients
- Breadstick dough, see page 111
- Extra-virgin olive oil, for brushing
- ¼ cup grated Parmesan

Equipment
- 13" x 18" baking pan
- Parchment paper

1 Prepare the dough.

2 Preheat the oven to 400°F (200°C).

3 Punch down the risen dough. Form it into a rough rectangle and use a pizza cutter to divide it into twelve equal portions.

4 Place the shaped breadsticks on a parchment-lined baking sheet, leaving some space between them. Brush them with extra-virgin olive oil and lightly sprinkle with the Parmesan.

5 Bake for 12–15 minutes or until the breadsticks turn golden brown.

Sicilian *Style*

Sicilian pizza originated in, you guessed it, Sicily, dating back to the 17th century. Rooted in Italy's traditional *sfincione*, this style emphasizes a focaccia-like crust that's both fluffy and crisp. Sicilian pizza stands out with its robust, thick, and often airy crust, which can hold up under a generous layer of tomato sauce and a variety of toppings. Typically, Sicilian pizzas are baked in square or rectangular pans, allowing the dough to rise and develop a satisfying texture. The regions that champion this style, especially New York and parts of New Jersey, have created their adaptations by using unique cheese blends, different sauces, and a variety of meats or vegetables. Other styles, like Cleveland and Brier Hill, take the spirit of a Sicilian and mesh it with round pans, creating styles all their own. Overall, a Sicilian pie will be light, airy, crispy, and ultra-satisfying.

Sicilian pizzas, featuring airy crusts and sweet sauce, may look heavy but are actually light and satisfying.

Traditional Sicilian

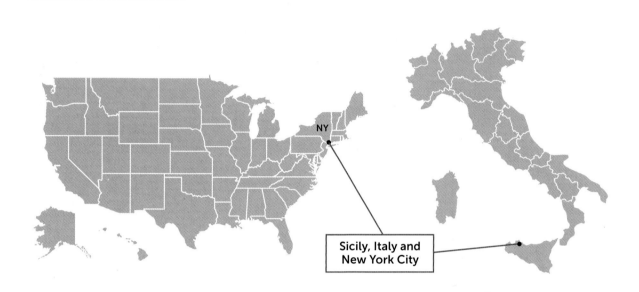

Sicily, Italy and
New York City

NY

The traditional or New York Sicilian is close to my heart. It's very close to the grandma pie I grew up on (see page 134), but a bit thicker due to the double rise. Light yet crisp, cheesy and savory, this pizza is one you need to master. Sicilian pizza originated in the Italian region of Sicily. It dates back to the 17th century and is characterized by its thick, spongy crust, with original versions often being topped with tomatoes, onions, anchovies, and herbs. Unlike traditional Neapolitan pizza, Sicilian pizza is typically baked in a rectangular pan. This style of pizza was brought to the United States by Sicilian immigrants in the early 20th century, where it gained popularity, especially in New York City.

SICILIAN DOUGH

MAKES ONE 14" X 14" PIZZA OR ONE 13" X 18" BREAD

Ingredients

- 3¼ cups (440g) **bread flour**
- 1¼ cups (296mL) **bottled water, warmed to 100°F (38°C)**
- 1 tablespoon (12g) **sugar**
- 2 teaspoons (6g) **active dry yeast**
- 2 teaspoons (12g) **table salt**
- 3 tablespoons (42g) **olive oil**

1 In your stand mixer or large bowl, gently combine the water, sugar, yeast, and 1 cup of the flour. Let stand for 5 minutes.

2 Following the rest period, begin to mix using the hook attachment on low or with well-oiled hands. Gradually pour in the remaining flour, salt, and oil. Mix for 5 minutes on medium-low speed or knead by hand for 10 minutes. The dough will be quite sticky.

3 Place the dough in a large, greased bowl. Let it rise on the counter for 2 hours or until doubled in size, then in the fridge overnight or for up to 3 days.

4 Remove the dough from the fridge 4 hours before cooking and let it come to room temperature.

SICILIAN SAUCE

MAKES ONE 14" X 14" PIZZA

Ingredients

- 2 tablespoons **olive oil**
- 3 tablespoons **tomato paste**
- 2 cloves **garlic, minced**
- 1½ cups **crushed tomatoes**
- 1 teaspoon **Italian seasoning**

1 On pizza day, combine the olive oil, tomato paste, and garlic in a small saucepan over medium heat. Cook, stirring constantly, for 3 minutes.

2 Add the crushed tomatoes, Italian seasoning, and a pinch of salt. Bring the sauce to a gentle simmer, stirring well to incorporate the tomato paste.

3 Simmer on low for 10 minutes, stirring frequently, then set it aside to cool until you're ready to cook.

Classic Sicilian Pizza

Here is the original style we all know and love—developed out of the original sfincione. If you don't have a Sicilian pizza pan (which is usually metal, 14" x 14", and 1"–2" tall), a baking sheet will work, as well. Just be sure to check for doneness often, as cooking times will vary. Also note that there are two camps of Sicilian pizza making: cheese first or sauce first. Since I grew up with sauce, then cheese, that is how we will start; if you prefer the opposite, check out some of the variants.

Ingredients

- Sicilian dough, see page 123
- Sicilian sauce, see page 123
- 12 ounces mozzarella cheese, sliced
- 2 tablespoons grated Parmesan
- 2 tablespoons grated Romano

Equipment

- 13" x 18" baking pan
- Large sauté pan
- Olive oil for greasing

This is one of the pies I grew up on, and one of the first things I learned how to make. It has the perfect balance of airy crust, crunchy exterior, and soft cheese-laden center.

1 Remove the prepared dough from the refrigerator 4 hours before cooking and let it come to room temperature.

2 Prepare the sauce.

3 Grease the pan with olive oil, then transfer the dough into it. Spread the dough into an even layer, pressing it into the corners. Cover and let the dough proof in the pan for 2 hours.

4 After proofing, preheat the oven to 450°F (**230°C**).

5 Using your fingertips, gently deflate any large bubbles or raised spots in the dough.

6 Spread a thin layer of the sauce on the pizza (½ cup of sauce is a good amount) and parbake (partially bake) for 8 minutes.

With a rise of only a few hours and a single baking step, this presto version is the Sicilian for when you need homemade pizza now!

7 Once parbaked, carefully remove the pizza from the pan and let it cool slightly. Re-oil the baking pan with 2–3 more tablespoons of olive oil.

8 Top the pizza with the remaining sauce and slices of cheese, then finish with the Parmesan and Romano.

9 Place the pizza back into the warm pan and bake for another 8–12 minutes or until the crust is deeply crisp and the cheese is golden. Remove from the pan, cut into squares, and serve once cooled enough that you won't burn the roof of your mouth.

Presto Sicilian

Sicilian pizzas are amazing, but we don't always have days to spare when pizza cravings hit and we need pizza on the table. This quick-rise (*presto*=Italian for "quick") Sicilian dough is my answer to same-day pizza desires. Other than the dough, use the same toppings and equipment as the classic Sicilian.

MAKES ONE 14" X 14" PIZZA

Presto Sicilian Dough Ingredients

- 3¼ cups (440g) **bread flour**
- 1¼ cups (296mL) **bottled water, warmed to 100°F (38°C)**
- 1½ tablespoons (18g) **sugar**
- 1 tablespoon (9g) **instant yeast**
- 2 teaspoons (12g) **table salt**
- 1 tablespoon (14g) **olive oil, plus more for greasing**

1 In your stand mixer or large bowl, gently combine the water, sugar, yeast, and 1 cup of the flour. Let rest for 5 minutes.

2 Following the rest period, begin to mix using the hook attachment on low or with well-oiled hands. Gradually pour in the remaining flour, salt, and oil. Mix for 5 minutes on medium-low speed or knead by hand for 10 minutes. The dough will be quite sticky.

3 Place the dough in a large, greased bowl. Let it rise on the counter for 2 hours. While the dough rises, make the Sicilian sauce (page 123).

4 Once the dough has risen in the bowl, grease the pan with olive oil, then transfer the dough into it. Spread the dough into an even layer, pressing it into the corners. If the dough is springy, cover and let it relax for 5 minutes before trying again. Cover and let the dough proof in the pan for 2 hours.

5 After proofing, preheat the oven to 450°F (230°C).

6 Using your fingertips, gently deflate any large bubbles or raised spots in the dough.

7 Spread a thin layer of the sauce on the pizza (½ cup of sauce is a good amount), add the cheeses, then follow with four thin, diagonal stripes of sauce.

8 Bake for 12–15 minutes or until the crust is deeply crisp and the cheese is golden. Remove from the pan, cut into squares, and serve once cooled enough that you won't burn the roof of your mouth.

Focaccia Bread

The Sicilian dough can also be morphed to make incredible focaccia bread. Here I find that using the baking sheet rather than the Sicilian pan gives better results. Light yet delightfully oily, this is a fantastic appetizer, sandwich bread, or late-night snack!

Light, crisp, and oily (in the best way), this is a go-to bread to keep on hand for regular meals and special occasions.

Ingredients

- Sicilian dough, see page 123
- 4 tablespoons olive oil
- 1 teaspoon flaky sea salt

Equipment

- 13" x 18" baking pan

1 Remove the prepared dough from the refrigerator 4 hours before cooking and let it come to room temperature.

2 Grease the pan with 1 tablespoon of the olive oil, then transfer the dough into it. Spread the dough into an even layer, pressing it into the corners. Cover and let the dough proof in the pan for 3 hours.

3 After proofing, preheat the oven to 450°F (230°C).

4 Using your fingertips, gently make slight divots in the dough to distribute large bubbles and to make mini wells for the olive oil to fill in.

5 Gently pour on the remaining olive oil and bake for 12–14 minutes or until just golden.

6 Once cooked, remove the focaccia from the pan, top it with the sea salt, and serve it either warm or at room temperature.

Garlic Focaccia Bread

What's better than focaccia bread? Garlic focaccia bread! This bread eats somewhere between a classic focaccia, garlic bread, and naan, with the sharp garlic and fruity olive oil intermingling on the fluffy bread base. By the way, this bread makes the world's finest BLTs (just in case you happen to be a fan of mind-blowing sandwiches).

Garlic bread 2.0. If you want a cheesier bite, add in a few slices of provolone right before baking.

Ingredients

- Sicilian dough, see page 123
- 4 tablespoons olive oil
- 5 cloves garlic, minced
- 1 ounce Romano cheese, grated
- 1 teaspoon flaky sea salt
- 1 tablespoon fresh parsley

Equipment

- 13" x 18" baking pan

1 Remove the prepared dough from the refrigerator 4 hours before cooking and let it come to room temperature.

2 Grease the pan with 1 tablespoon of the olive oil, then transfer the dough into it. Spread the dough into an even layer, pressing it into the corners. Cover and let the dough proof in the pan for 3 hours.

3 After proofing, preheat the oven to 450°F (230°C).

4 Using your fingertips, gently make slight divots in the dough to distribute large bubbles and to make mini wells for the olive oil to fill in.

5 Gently pour on the remaining olive oil, add the garlic and Romano cheese, and bake for 12–14 minutes or until just golden.

6 Once cooked, remove the focaccia from the pan, top it with the sea salt and parsley, and serve it either warm or at room temperature.

Sfincione

The original old-world version of the Sicilian, the sfincione is a spongy, focaccia-like crust topped with a sharp tomato sauce and anchovies. It is amazing at room temperature served with a sharp glass of prosecco. While the traditional features a hard Sicilian cheese known as *caciocavallo*, we will use the more readily available Pecorino Romano and Parmigiano-Reggiano. Quality matters on the breadcrumbs you use—if your brand isn't outstanding, make your own or procure some from an Italian deli.

Ingredients

- Sicilian dough, see page 123
- 3 tablespoons olive oil
- 1 onion, sliced thin
- 1 tablespoon fresh oregano, plus more for topping
- 1 teaspoon red pepper flakes

- 4 anchovy filets, minced
- 1 cup passata or canned cherry tomatoes
- 1 ounce grated Parmigiano-Reggiano
- 2 ounces grated Pecorino Romano
- ½ cup Italian breadcrumbs

Equipment

- 13" x 18" baking pan
- Large sauté pan

1 Remove the prepared dough from the refrigerator 4 hours before cooking and let it come to room temperature.

2 Grease the pan with 1 tablespoon of the olive oil, then transfer the dough into it. Spread the dough into an even layer, pressing it into the corners. Cover and let the dough proof in the pan for 2 hours.

3 While the dough rises, heat the remaining 2 tablespoons of olive oil and the onions in a large sauté pan over medium-high heat. Continue to cook, stirring frequently, until the onions are a deep golden brown, about 20 minutes total.

4 Add the oregano, red pepper flakes, and anchovies and cook, stirring constantly, until fragrant, about 30 seconds. Add the tomatoes and stir to combine.

5 Bring to a simmer, then reduce to low and cook, stirring often, until very thick, about 30 minutes. Once cooked, remove from the heat, cool, and set aside.

6 Once the dough is risen, preheat the oven to 450°F (230°C).

7 Top the dough with the sauce, Parmigiano-Reggiano, Pecorino Romano, breadcrumbs, and a sprinkle of oregano.

8 Bake for 18–20 minutes or until the crust is brown and the tomatoes have just dried.

Don't leave the anchovies off of this one! The flavor will be savory and salty, and not at all fishy. This is one of the oldest recipes in the book, and it just would not be the same without that briny bite.

Cup and Char Sicilian Pizza

There are many Sicilian pizza masters on this planet, but few embody and embrace the style quite like World Pizza Champion John Gristina. At his pizzeria, Pizza Fenice in Pelham, New York, he is making his pies the right way, having worked with and trained some of the best pizza makers in the world. The result is a flawless slice that I dream of daily. While he features many, many different pizzas, from classics to wild creations (his Pastrami Reuben is 10/10 perfect), I fell in love with his classic pepperoni. The secret is the use of "cup and char" pepperoni, a style of pepperoni that curls up at the edges and forms a cup shape when cooked, often with crispy, charred edges. This effect is achieved because of the specific type of casing used and the fat content in the pepperoni. The higher fat content and natural casing allow the pepperoni slices to curl and char, creating a unique texture and flavor that is particularly popular on pizzas. This style of pepperoni is favored for its crispy edges and the way it holds small pools of oil, adding to its savory appeal. While this recipe only adds one ingredient to the traditional Sicilian, the depth and layers of flavor cannot be overstated!

Ingredients

- Sicilian dough, see page 123
- Sicilian sauce, see page 123
- 12 ounces mozzarella cheese, sliced
- 2 tablespoons grated Parmesan
- 2 tablespoons grated Romano
- 6 ounces cup and char pepperoni

Equipment

- 14" x 14" Sicilian pan
- Olive oil for the pan

1 Remove the prepared dough from the refrigerator 4 hours before cooking and let it come to room temperature.

2 Prepare the sauce.

3 Grease the pan with olive oil, then transfer the dough into it. Spread the dough into an even layer, pressing it into the corners. Cover and let the dough proof in the pan for 2 hours.

4 After proofing, preheat the oven to 450°F (230°C).

5 Using your fingertips, gently deflate any large bubbles or raised spots in the dough.

6 Spread a thin layer of the sauce on the pizza (½ cup of sauce is a good amount) and add 1 ounce of the pepperoni, then parbake (partially bake) for 8 minutes.

7 Once parbaked, carefully remove the pizza from the pan and let it cool slightly. Re-oil the baking pan with 2–3 more tablespoons of olive oil.

8 Top the pizza with the remaining sauce and slices of cheese, the Parmesan and Romano, and the remaining pepperoni.

9 Place the pizza back into the warm pan and bake for another 8–12 minutes or until the crust is deeply crisp and the cheese is golden. Remove from the pan, cut into squares, and serve once cooled enough that you won't burn the roof of your mouth.

My take on the cup and char pepperoni-laden Sicilian is ready to eat as soon as it cools—so no need to wait!

■ *Inspiration:* John Gristina's pizzas are masterpieces. Note the crisp pepperoni, the smooth cheese, and the texture on that crust.

Sesame Sicilian Pizza

Finishing our Sicilian journey, we will add one more wrinkle: sesame seeds. This recipe elevates the classic Sicilian pizza by incorporating both crispy cup and char pepperoni and thin-sliced pepperoni, adding a flavorful punch and a unique texture. Additionally, the sprinkle of sesame seeds on the crust introduces a nutty, aromatic note that complements the robust toppings perfectly. Finally, this version layers sauce, then cheese, then sauce, which many prefer for a Sicilian!

Ingredients

- Sicilian dough, see page 123
- Sicilian sauce, see page 123
- 12 ounces mozzarella cheese, sliced
- 2 tablespoons grated Parmesan
- 2 tablespoons grated Romano
- 3 tablespoons sesame seeds
- 2 ounces thin-cut pepperoni
- 4 ounces cup and char pepperoni
- 10 basil leaves, torn

Equipment

- 14" x 14" Sicilian pan
- Olive oil for the pan

1 Remove the prepared dough from the refrigerator 4 hours before cooking and let it come to room temperature.

2 Prepare the sauce.

3 Grease the pan with olive oil, then transfer the dough into it. Spread the dough into an even layer, pressing it into the corners. Cover and let the dough proof in the pan for 2 hours.

4 After proofing, preheat the oven to 450°F (230°C).

5 Using your fingertips, gently deflate any large bubbles or raised spots in the dough.

6 Spread a thin layer of the sauce on the pizza (½ cup is a good amount) and gently press the sesame seeds around the rim, then parbake (partially bake) for 8 minutes.

7 Once parbaked, carefully remove the pizza from the pan and let it cool slightly. Raise the temperature on the oven to 475°F (245°C). Re-oil the baking pan with 2–3 more tablespoons of olive oil.

8 Top the pizza with the slices of cheese, thin pepperoni, dollops of the remaining sauce, the Parmesan and Romano, and the cup and char pepperoni.

9 Place the pizza back into the warm pan and bake for another 8–12 minutes or until the crust is deeply crisp and the cheese is golden. Remove from the pan, cut into squares, garnish with the basil, and serve once cooled enough that you won't burn the roof of your mouth.

Inspiration: A nutty crust is the perfect complement to Jim Henry's pizza and its slightly caramelized sauce.

Grandma

New York City
NY

This pizza most closely represents the pizza I had at home growing up . . . and for good reason. This pizza was thought to originate from Italian American immigrants in the early 1900s. Seeing as how I have a Sicilian grandmother, this all tracks. This dough is also very similar to the dough found in the original *Joy of Cooking* cookbook, which, you guessed it, was the midcentury cooking bible. It all comes together as the quintessential family pizza—quick, resourceful, and as tasty as can be.

Gluten-Free Alternative

Gluten-free? Try making any of the grandma pizzas with a double batch of the gluten-free classic pan dough on page 71 in a 13" x 18" pan. Follow the instructions in the grandma pie recipe on page 135.

GRANDMA DOUGH

MAKES ONE 14" X 14" OR 13" X 18" PIZZA

Ingredients

- **3½ cups** (473g) **bread flour**
- **1¼ cups** (296mL) **bottled water, warmed to 100°F** (38°C)
- **1 tablespoon** (12g) **sugar**
- **2 teaspoons** (6g) **active dry yeast**
- **1½ teaspoons** (9g) **table salt**
- **1 tablespoon** (14g) **olive oil**

1 In your stand mixer or large bowl, gently combine the water, sugar, yeast, and 1 cup of the flour. Let stand for 5 minutes.

2 Following the rest period, begin to mix using the hook attachment on low or with well-oiled hands. Gradually pour in the remaining flour, salt, and oil. Mix for 5 minutes on medium-low speed or knead by hand for 10 minutes. The dough will be quite sticky.

3 Place the dough in a large, greased bowl. Let it rise on the counter for 2 hours or until doubled in size, then in the fridge for at least 4 hours, up to overnight.

4 Remove the dough from the fridge 4 hours before cooking and let it come to room temperature.

Grandma Pie

A nod to the Sicilian in general shape, the grandma pie has some distinct differences. The dough is a quicker rise, and unlike its cousin, it is not risen in the pan, but rather baked instantly. This results in a delightfully dense and crisp dough that, mixed with the oil, is almost biscuit-like. We also will be using the more readily available 13" x 18" pan rather than the more specialized 14" x 14" Sicilian pan. Also note that putting the sauce on top would be traditional for a grandma-style pie, but I'm starting with my own grandmother's sauce-first method.

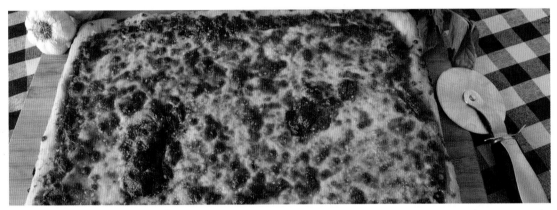

The other pie I grew up on (depending on who was cooking), this pizza is a bit denser than a Sicilian, but loaded with traditional flavors and a bready crust.

Ingredients

- Grandma dough, see page 134
- 2 tablespoons olive oil
- 2 cloves garlic, minced
- 3 tablespoons tomato paste
- 1⅓ cups crushed tomatoes
- 1 teaspoon fresh oregano
- 12 ounces mozzarella cheese, grated
- 2 tablespoons grated Parmesan

Equipment

- 13" x 18" baking pan
- Olive oil for pan

1 Remove the prepared dough from the refrigerator 4 hours before cooking and let it come to room temperature.

2 While the dough rises, heat the olive oil in a saucepot over medium heat. Add the garlic, tomato paste, and a pinch of salt, then cook, stirring continuously, for 3 minutes.

3 Add in the crushed tomatoes and oregano and bring to just a simmer. Cool and set aside until you're ready to cook.

4 Liberally oil the baking sheet, wiping off the excess with a towel. Preheat the oven to 450°F (230°C).

5 Roll the dough into the shape of a baking sheet, using flour on the surface as needed to prevent sticking.

6 Transfer the dough to the pan, then use your knuckles to gently press the dough into the sides of the baking pan.

7 Top the pizza with the sauce, mozzarella cheese, and a heavy sprinkle of the Parmesan.

8 Bake for 16–20 minutes or until very brown on all sides. Remove from the pan, cut into squares, and devour.

Grandma Margherita Pie

It is an honor to feature and discuss various pizza masters within this book. When I first met Dominic Russo at Squares & Fare in Somers Point, New Jersey, I had a hunch he was a pizza legend. Then, after I tried his pizza, my suspicions were confirmed. Dominic makes a perfect grandma slice—crisp, bready, but completely balanced. He does abide by traditional grandma rules, with sauce on the top, cheese right out to the edge, and that 14" x 14" pan. He also prides himself on using local New Jersey tomatoes, basil, and oregano, treating each with a gardener's level of care. I have many, many favorites of his, but we need to start with a tribute to his classic and wildly flavorful Margherita pie.

Inspiration: Dominic is a master. Note the charred crust, the perfectly layered cheeses, and the sauce made from his local tomatoes.

Ingredients

- Grandma dough, see page 134
- 2 tablespoons olive oil, plus more for drizzling
- 1 cup crushed tomatoes
- 1 tablespoon roasted garlic
- 10 ounces mozzarella cheese, sliced
- 8 basil leaves
- 1 ounce Parmesan, shaved

Equipment

- 14" x 14" Sicilian pan
- Olive oil for pan

1 Remove the prepared dough from the refrigerator 4 hours before cooking and let it come to room temperature.

2 Combine the olive oil, crushed tomatoes, roasted garlic, and a pinch of salt.

3 Liberally oil the pan and preheat the oven to 450°F (230°C).

4 Form the dough into the shape of the pan, using flour on the surface as needed to prevent sticking.

5 Transfer the dough to the pan, then use your knuckles to gently press the dough into the sides of the pan.

6 Top the pizza with slices of cheese out to the edge, then dollops of the crushed tomato mixture, and finally basil leaves.

7 Bake for 16–20 minutes or until very brown on all sides. Remove from the pan and garnish with the shaved Parmesan and a drizzle of olive oil. Cut into squares and devour.

Grandma Sausage and Ricotta Pie

One of the beautiful aspects of a grandma pie is its ability to handle bold and delicate flavors alike. Another pie Dominic Russo of Squares & Fare has featured combines both: spicy Italian sausage and gentle ricotta cheese. The result is a harmony of flavors and textures that is beyond compare. Trust me when I say this particular recipe is a can't miss. Our at-home version uses whipped ricotta, which is light and the perfect pizza topping. Also note that the hotter the sausage the better for this flavor-packed feast.

Inspiration: Spicy and savory sausage, light ricotta, and fresh basil . . . Dominic's creation is a pie I dream about.

Ingredients
- Grandma dough, see page 134
- 3 tablespoons olive oil, divided, plus more for drizzling
- 2 cloves garlic, minced
- 1 cup crushed tomatoes
- 1 teaspoon Italian seasoning
- 2 tablespoons tomato paste
- 2 links hot Italian sausage
- 10 ounces mozzarella cheese, sliced
- 1 ounce grated Parmesan
- 8 basil leaves
- 1 cup whipped ricotta cheese

Equipment
- 14" x 14" Sicilian pan
- Olive oil for pan
- Large frying pan

1 Remove the prepared dough from the refrigerator 4 hours before cooking and let it come to room temperature.

2 While the dough rises, heat 2 tablespoons of the olive oil in a saucepot over medium heat. Add the garlic, tomato paste, and a pinch of salt, then cook, stirring continuously, for 3 minutes.

3 Add in the crushed tomatoes and Italian seasoning and bring to just a simmer. Cool and set aside until you're ready to cook.

4 Place a large frying pan over medium heat. Slice the links of sausage into six to eight rounds, then gently remove the casing. Heat the remaining tablespoon of olive oil in the pan until it just shimmers, then cook the sausage chunks for 7–8 minutes or until browned, stirring often. Remove and cool until you're ready to cook.

5 Liberally oil the baking sheet and preheat the oven to 450°F (230°C).

6 Form the dough into the shape of the pan, using flour on the surface as needed to prevent sticking.

7 Transfer the dough to the pan, then use your knuckles to gently press the dough into the sides of the pan.

8 Top the pizza with slices of cheese out to the edge, dollops of the sauce, the sausage, and the grated Parmesan.

9 Bake for 16–20 minutes or until very brown on all sides. Remove from the pan and garnish with the basil, dollops of ricotta, and a drizzle of olive oil. Cut into squares and devour.

Grandma Tomato Pie

The grandma dough is one of my favorites because of its versatility. The thicker dough can handle more toppings, of course, but it can also support more sauce as well. We can mash up a grandma pie with the Philly tomato pie (see page 147) to create a truly interesting slice. As we have shown elsewhere in this book, while the ingredients are almost identical to a plain cheese pizza, the technique is what creates something entirely new!

Inspiration: The sauce on top of Jim Henry's pie becomes a little sticky, like a Chicago deep dish, adding both a sweetness and a textural counterpoint to the crust.

Ingredients

- Grandma dough, see page 134
- 1½ cups crushed tomatoes
- 10 ounces mozzarella cheese, sliced
- 8 basil leaves
- 1 ounce grated Parmesan

Equipment

- 14" x 14" Sicilian pan
- Olive oil for pan

1 Remove the prepared dough from the refrigerator 4 hours before cooking and let it come to room temperature.

2 Liberally oil the baking sheet and preheat the oven to 450°F (230°C).

3 Form the dough into the shape of the pan, using flour on the surface as needed to prevent sticking.

4 Transfer the dough to the pan, then use your knuckles to gently press the dough into the sides of the pan.

5 Top the pizza with slices of cheese out to ½" from the edge, sprinkle on the Parmesan, and completely cover the cheese with the crushed tomatoes, then the basil leaves.

6 Bake for 16–20 minutes or until very brown on all sides and the sauce has just begun to caramelize. Remove from the pan, cut into squares, and devour.

Taglio

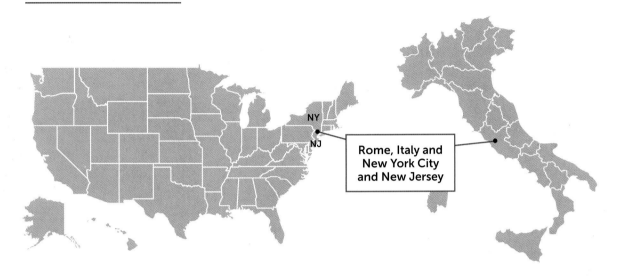

Rome, Italy and
New York City
and New Jersey

Pizza al taglio, or "pizza by the cut," is one of the quintessential Italian pizzas, most popular in and around Rome. It's a cross between a modern puffy Sicilian and a Neapolitan. In the states, this pizza is generally found in the New York/New Jersey area, and the offerings are often loaded with premium toppings. When making this recipe at home, the possibilities are endless; just be sure to cut it into rectangles and enjoy with a chianti for maximum effect.

TAGLIO DOUGH

MAKES ONE 9" X 13" PIZZA

Ingredients

- 1¾ cups (225g) **bread flour**
- ⅔ cup plus 1 tablespoon (160ml) **bottled water**
- 1 teaspoon (3g) **active dry yeast**
- 1 tablespoon (14g) **olive oil, plus more for drizzling**
- 1 teaspoon (6g) **table salt**

1 In a small bowl or cup, combine the yeast, water, and oil.

2 In a very large mixing bowl, combine the flour and salt and make a well in the middle.

3 Gently add the water mixture and slowly stir in the flour. Fold in all of the flour and work to combine.

4 Knead for 8–10 minutes until the dough comes together, then form it into a ball. Drizzle the dough with a bit more olive oil.

5 Cover the dough and let it rise on the counter for 4–6 hours, punching it down halfway, then place the dough in the fridge for 48 hours.

6 Remove the dough from the fridge 3 hours before cooking and bring the dough to room temperature.

Taglio Margherita

This recipe is based on a recipe from a Roman chef friend of mine, so you know it is perfectly authentic. Think of this as a base for whatever toppings you can conceive of, as there are very few rules when it comes to al taglio pizza. Personally, however, starting with a classic Margherita is a wonderful choice to fully showcase what this dough can do.

Ingredients
- Taglio dough, see page 139
- ⅔ cup passata
- 6 ounces fresh mozzarella, sliced
- ½ cup halved cherry tomatoes
- 10 basil leaves
- Olive oil, for drizzling

Equipment
- 9" x 13" baking pan
- Olive oil for pan

1 Remove the prepared dough from the refrigerator 3 hours before cooking and let it come to room temperature.

2 Form the ball into a 9" x 13" rectangle.

3 Liberally oil the baking sheet and preheat the oven to 475°F (245°C). Place a rack in the lowest third of the oven.

4 Transfer the dough to the pan, ensuring that it is even all around.

5 Top the pizza with the passata, a pinch of salt, the mozzarella, then the cherry tomatoes.

6 Bake for 16–20 minutes or until crisp. Garnish with the basil leaves and a drizzle of olive oil, then cut and enjoy.

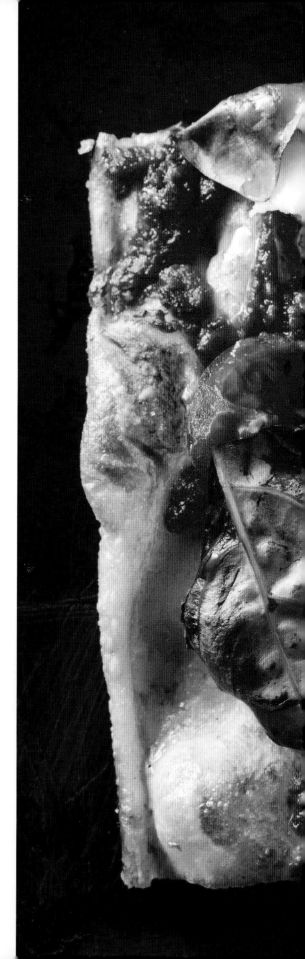

This is the classic Roman slice, where the Margherita toppings meet al taglio street style.

Salami and Tomato Taglio

There was one combination of toppings I saw everywhere when in Rome. Salami and tomatoes were very prevalent, and these pies usually did not feature any sauce layer. Another traditional element was the cheese—many featured a combination of aged cheese (Pecorino Romano) and young cheeses (Pecorino Toscano). To simplify our pie, we will keep the Pecorino Romano but sub in provolone for the Toscano. An approachable step to our taglio journey, this pizza is also perfect picnic lunch fare.

Ingredients

- Taglio dough, see page 139
- 2 ounces Pecorino Romano cheese, grated
- 6 ounces provolone, grated
- 1 tomato, sliced thin
- 1 pinch of salt
- 2 ounces salami, sliced thin
- Olive oil, for drizzling

Equipment

- 9" x 13" baking pan
- Vegetable oil for pan

1 Remove the prepared dough from the refrigerator 3 hours before cooking and let it come to room temperature.

2 Form the ball into a 9" x 13" rectangle.

3 Liberally oil the baking sheet and preheat the oven to 475°F (245°C). Place a rack in the lowest third of the oven.

4 Transfer the dough to the pan, ensuring that it is even all around.

5 Top the pizza with the tomato, then the Pecorino Romano, then the provolone, a pinch of salt, and finally the salami.

6 Bake for 16–20 minutes or until crisp. Finish with a heavy drizzle of olive oil.

The Roman version of a pepperoni pizza. Salami and tomatoes sub in for the tomato sauce and pepperoni, adding fresh deli flavors to a pizza. You can also add a few black olives and fresh basil if you're looking for an additional kick.

Quattro Formaggi

Four cheeses, one slice—need I say more? No, but I will anyway. Our version is a *bianca*, or "white", meaning it has no tomato sauce. The mix of cheeses used varies depending on the region, but mozzarella is usually the star, and gorgonzola, fontina, and Parmigiano-Reggiano are also popular. I really enjoy this mix, so I've gone with this lineup. If you want to branch out, try using asiagos, Romanos, or other blue cheeses, just keep the total amount of cheese under 8 ounces.

The cheeses on this one play with each other perfectly—the smooth mozzarella and fontina, the funky gorgonzola, and the aged Parmigiano-Reggiano create a harmonic chord of flavors that is unrivaled.

Ingredients

- Taglio dough, see page 139
- 1 ounce gorgonzola, crumbled
- 1 ounce Parmigiano-Reggiano, shaved
- 4 ounces mozzarella, grated
- 2 ounces fontina, grated
- Olive oil, for drizzling

Equipment

- 9" x 13" baking pan
- Vegetable oil for pan

1 Remove the prepared dough from the refrigerator 3 hours before cooking and let it come to room temperature.

2 Form the ball into a 9" x 13" rectangle.

3 Liberally oil the baking sheet and preheat the oven to 475°F (245°C). Place a rack in the lowest third of the oven.

4 Transfer the dough to the pan, ensuring that it is even all around.

5 Top the pizza with the gorgonzola, then the Parmigiano-Reggiano, then the mozzarella, and finally the fontina.

6 Bake for 16–20 minutes or until crisp. Finish with a heavy drizzle of olive oil.

Spinach and Artichoke Roman

This book is fortunate enough to feature many world-class pizza artisans, and when I think of Rob Cervoni, world class probably doesn't do him enough justice. A *Chopped* champion and 2022 "Rising Star of Pizza," Rob is arguably one of the best pizza makers on the planet. Rob opened Taglio Pizzeria in Long Island, the first Roman-style pizzeria in the area. Taglio does everything just as it's done on the streets of Rome. There are two slices at Taglio that I find especially incredible, the first being the Carciofi E' Spinaci (shown in the top right of the inspiration photo below). Think of this as a Roman spinach and artichoke dip, only fancier. Our version is inspired by Rob's masterpiece and is everything you could dream it would be. The key here is controlling the moisture—ensure that the spinach is completely cooked and as dry as possible.

This recipe requires cooked, dry spinach to create perfection and avoid a soggy slice.

Inspiration: Rob Cervoni makes some of the best taglio slices on the planet, and here is Exhibit A. Known for his adventurous topping combinations (inspired by familiar Italian ingredients and flavors), his taglio landscape is culinary gold.

Ingredients

- Taglio dough, see page 139
- 6 ounces provolone, grated
- ½ cup spinach, cooked and drained
- ⅓ cup artichoke hearts, packed in oil
- 2 ounces Romano cheese, grated
- Olive oil, for drizzling

Equipment

- 9" x 13" baking pan
- Vegetable oil for pan

1 Remove the prepared dough from the refrigerator 3 hours before cooking and let it come to room temperature.

2 Form the ball into a 9" x 13" rectangle.

3 Liberally oil the baking sheet and preheat the oven to 475°F (245°C). Place a rack in the lowest third of the oven.

4 Transfer the dough to the pan, ensuring that it is even all around.

5 Top the pizza with the provolone, then the spinach, then the artichokes, and finally the Romano.

6 Bake for 16–20 minutes or until crisp. Finish with a heavy drizzle of olive oil.

Il Fungo

Another slice of Roman pizza I adore is a mushroom-laden slice bursting with umami goodness. Taglio's version, the Truffle Funghi, is a masterpiece of mushroom-based flavors. Our take uses truffle oil, which is a bit easier to find (and afford) than pure truffles. This is a rich slice, but I promise you'll have no issue having seconds or thirds.

This is a mushroom lover's delight, in which the earthy flavors have a chance to shine against the soft mozzarella.

Ingredients
- Taglio dough, see page 139
- 2 ounces Romano cheese, grated
- 6 ounces mozzarella, grated
- 1 cup sliced and sautéed cremini mushrooms
- 1 tablespoon truffle oil for drizzling

Equipment
- 9" x 13" baking pan
- Vegetable oil for pan

1 Remove the prepared dough from the refrigerator 3 hours before cooking and let it come to room temperature.

2 Form the ball into a 9" x 13" rectangle.

3 Liberally oil the baking sheet and preheat the oven to 475°F (245°C). Place a rack in the lowest third of the oven.

4 Transfer the dough to the pan, ensuring that it is even all around.

5 Top the pizza with the Romano, then the mozzarella, and finally the mushrooms.

6 Bake for 16–20 minutes or until crisp. Finish with a drizzle of truffle oil.

Philly Tomato Pie

Philly tomato pie is sublime, though closer to perhaps a bread than a pizza. This tracks, since it is more often found in restaurants that started as bakeries rather than pizza shops. The dough has clear roots in Sicily, especially given the rectangular shape. Best served as a main or a killer appetizer, this dough is akin to a focaccia without the bench proof. The dough is complex and moist, which is a perfect foil to the sweet tomato sauce. The Romano at the end gives the tomato pie a tang that cannot be replicated.

PHILLY DOUGH

MAKES ONE 9" X 13" PIZZA

Ingredients

- 3½ cups (472g) **bread flour**
- 1⅓ cups (315mL) **filtered water, warmed to 100°F (38°C)**
- 2 tablespoons (28g) **olive oil**
- 1½ teaspoons (5g) **instant yeast**
- 1½ teaspoons (9g) **table salt**

1 In a small bowl or cup, combine the yeast, water, and oil.

2 In a very large mixing bowl, combine the flour and salt and make a well in the middle.

3 Gently add the water mixture and slowly stir in the flour. Fold in all of the flour and work to combine.

4 Knead for 8–10 minutes until the dough comes together, then form it into a ball. Drizzle the dough with a bit more olive oil.

5 Let the dough rise on the counter for 4–6 hours, punching it down halfway, then place the dough in the fridge for 8 to 24 hours.

6 Remove the dough from the fridge 4 hours before cooking and let it come to room temperature.

Gluten-Free Alternative

Gluten-free? Try making any of the Philly pizzas with a double batch of the gluten-free classic pan dough on page 71 in a 13" x 18" pan. Follow the instructions in the Philly tomato pie recipe on page 148.

Philly Tomato Pie

Gaeta's Italian Bakery in Philadelphia, Pennsylvania, is the spot I think of when I imagine a Philly tomato pie. A proper Italian-style bakery, this spot has been making classics since 1932, like their pan-baked tomato pies, stuffed breads, stromboli, and traditional pizzas. Here we will explore and present our version of their classic. This is a straightforward tomato pie—no muss, fuss, or mozzarella required.

Straightforward and just a little fruity, my homage to the Philly classic slice has a caramelized tomato edge (which is by far my favorite place to start eating).

Inspiration: Sweet, tangy, and bready, this is a wonderful creation by Gaeta's, which is considered to be as much of a bakery as a pizzeria. The crushed tomatoes become a little sticky, fusing with the dough to create a very interesting combination.

Ingredients

- Philly dough, see page 147
- 2 cups crushed tomatoes
- 1 teaspoon dried oregano
- 1 teaspoon sugar
- ½ teaspoon salt
- 1 teaspoon red pepper flakes
- 3 tablespoons grated Romano
- 2 tablespoons olive oil

Equipment

- 13" x 18" metal pan
- Olive oil for pan

1 Sometime before pizza day, combine the crushed tomatoes, dried oregano, sugar, salt, and red pepper flakes (no need to cook). Keep cool until ready to cook.

2 Remove the prepared dough from the refrigerator 4 hours before cooking and let it come to room temperature.

3 Liberally oil the metal pan. Roll out the dough to the size of the pan, using flour as needed to prevent sticking. Then move the dough to the pan and let it rise for 1 hour.

4 Preheat the oven to 450°F (230°C). Gently dock the dough (poke holes into it to let steam release during baking) with a fork to knock down some of the larger bubbles.

5 Top the pizza with the sauce right out to the edge, sprinkle on the grated Romano, and finish with a drizzle of olive oil.

6 Bake for 20–24 minutes or until the crust is deeply golden and the sauce is just turning brick red, rotating halfway through. Let cool for 10 minutes and serve.

Philly Pepper Pie

The other Philly tomato pie we will cover . . . doesn't have any tomatoes in it. Instead, this "white" pie has loads of sweet roasted bell peppers and Romano cheese. The result is a unique but wildly interesting sheet that pairs perfectly with a glass of white and grilled chicken (or a cheesesteak). If there is a trick to our version of this classic pepper pie, it is the roasting of the peppers. The char brings a subtle smoky flavor that acts as a perfect foil for the savory dough. While the use of jarred peppers is tempting, this is a key step to this pie!

Roasting the peppers brings out the subtle smokiness, which ties the base flavors into the peppers perfectly.

■ **Inspiration:** With the fried peppers on the wonderful dough, Gaeta's creation eats like a stuffed pepper (though in many ways it's lighter).

Ingredients

- Philly dough, see page 147
- 3 bell peppers in different colors
- 1 tablespoon olive oil
- ½ teaspoon salt
- ¼ cup grated Pecorino Romano cheese

Equipment

- 13" x 18" metal pan
- Baking sheet
- Olive oil for pan

1 Remove the prepared dough from the refrigerator 4 hours before cooking and let it come to room temperature.

2 Liberally oil the metal pan. Roll out the dough to the size of the metal pan, using flour as needed to prevent sticking. Then move the dough to the pan and let it rise for 1 hour.

3 Preheat the oven to 450°F (230°C).

4 Cut the bell peppers in half lengthwise and remove the seeds and stems. Place the pepper halves on a baking sheet, skin side up, and lightly coat them with the olive oil and salt.

5 Roast the peppers for 20–25 minutes, or until the skins are charred and blistered. Remove the peppers from the oven, cool them, then slice them into strips.

6 Gently dock the dough (poke holes into it to let steam release during baking) with a fork to knock down some of the larger bubbles.

7 Top the dough with a sprinkle of grated Pecorino Romano, then layer on the sliced peppers.

8 Bake for 20–22 minutes or until the crust is deeply golden, rotating halfway through. Let cool for 10 minutes and serve.

Buffalo

The Buffalo pizza isn't a chicken wing on bread. Rather, this pizza is delightfully light and airy, akin to a pizza bread almost. The crust is focaccia-esque, though perhaps with less oil and appreciably thinner. Note the unusual technique: Starting with a high-hydration dough at first allows for a faster ferment, and folding in the flour after an hour helps the dough come together. The sauce is heavy on the garlic and a bit sweet, the opposite of other similar pies. While some Buffalo-area pizzerias use mozzarella, I find that provolone is more popular (and fits this pie better, in my opinion). Finally, the pepperoni is cut dangerously thick, adding a crisp texture that contrasts against the light crust. A dark horse pizza, move this pie to the top of your list!

BUFFALO-STYLE DOUGH

**MAKES ONE 14" X 14"
OR 16" ROUND PIZZA**

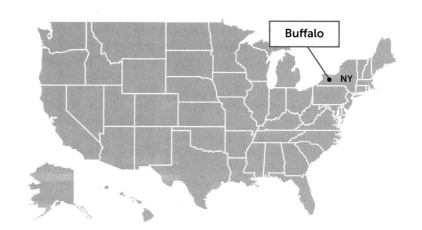

Ingredients

- **3¾ cups (500g) bread flour**
- **1⅓ cups (315mL) warm water**
- **1 tablespoon (12g) sugar**
- **2 teaspoons (6g) active dry yeast**
- **2 tablespoons (28g) shortening**
- **1½ teaspoons (9g) table salt**

1 In the bowl of a large mixer, add 1 cup of the flour and the water, sugar, and yeast. Combine and let sit for 10 minutes.

2 Using the hook attachment on low, slowly add the remaining flour, the shortening, and the salt.

3 Mix for 6 minutes, then remove the dough from the bowl and form it into a ball.

4 Let the dough rise for 4 hours on the counter, then 24–36 hours in the refrigerator.

5 Remove the dough from the fridge 4–6 hours before cooking to let it come to room temperature and finish rising.

Buffalo-Style Pepperoni Pizza

In 1978, the world was blessed when Carbone's Pizza first opened its doors in Buffalo, New York. Here, they still hand-cut pepperoni and grate cheese on the daily, and their passion shows through in every bite. The current owner, Nicholas Carbone, exudes the energy that only a lifelong pizzaiolo can, and speaking and learning from him was one of the best parts of writing this book. We start then with a pie in homage to their classic pepperoni, which is not your average pie. If there is a trick to this pizza, it is the thick-cut (or even better, hand-cut) pepperoni, which provides a textural component than cannot be beat.

Note that our version has a little more edge crust than the classic, which I find a bit easier to eat, but feel free to "over cheese" to create the traditional overflowing vibes.

Inspiration: I adore how Carbone's goes all-in with their pies. A signature of the style is the copious amounts of hand-cut pepperoni.

Ingredients

- Buffalo-style dough, see page 150
- 1 tablespoon olive oil
- 2 cloves of garlic, crushed
- 3 tablespoons tomato paste
- 1 cup crushed tomatoes
- 1 tablespoon Italian seasoning
- 6 ounces pepperoni, thick-cut
- 8 ounces provolone, grated
- 10 ounces mozzarella, grated
- 2 tablespoons grated Parmesan

Equipment

- 14" x 14" pizza pan or 16" round baking pan
- Olive oil for pan

1 Sometime before pizza day, add the olive oil and garlic to a saucepot over low heat. Sweat for 2 minutes, then add the tomato paste. Cook for 3–4 minutes to soften, then add the crushed tomatoes, Italian seasoning, and a pinch of salt. Raise the heat to a simmer and cook for 15 minutes. Keep cool until ready to cook.

2 Remove the dough from the fridge 4–6 hours before cooking.

3 Liberally oil the pan and preheat the oven to 475°F (245°C).

4 Roll out the dough to the size of the pan, using flour as needed to prevent sticking. Do not add a lip.

5 Transfer the dough to the pan and gently form dimples with your fingers.

6 Top the pizza with the sauce, provolone, mozzarella, and pepperoni. Push the cheese right out the edge if you want.

7 Bake for 12–16 minutes or until the crust is deeply golden. Remove from the oven, top with the grated Parmesan, cut into squares, and serve.

"Buffalo" Buffalo Pizza

Okay, I get it, you saw "Buffalo pizza" and you want **that** pizza. Luckily, Buffalo-style dough handles heat just as well as anything else, so this pie isn't a stretch in the slightest. When choosing a Buffalo sauce, err on the milder, more acidic side of the spectrum; you can always add chili flakes, but they've yet to invent a way to de-spice hot sauce.

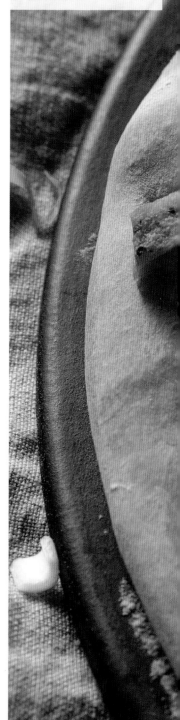

The ultimate gameday meal, the spicy tang of the buffalo sauce plays perfectly against this pizza's soft, slightly sweet crust. Try adding sliced red onion before you bake for another fresh flavor boost.

Ingredients

- Buffalo-style dough, see page 150
- 1 cup Buffalo sauce
- 1 tablespoon olive oil
- 5 cloves of garlic, crushed
- 6 ounces provolone, grated
- 8 ounces cheddar cheese, grated
- ¼ cup thinly sliced green onions
- 1 cup cooked and cubed chicken
- ¼ cup crumbled bleu cheese

Equipment

- 14" x 14" pizza pan or 16" round baking pan
- Olive oil for pan

1 Sometime before pizza day, add the olive oil and garlic to a saucepot over low heat. Sweat for 2 minutes, then add in the Buffalo sauce. Cook for 3–4 minutes to combine, then cool until ready to cook.

2 Remove the dough from the fridge 4–6 hours before cooking.

3 Liberally oil the pan and preheat the oven to 475°F (245°C).

4 Roll out the dough to the size of the pan, using flour as needed to prevent sticking. Add a slight lip (this is needed since the Buffalo sauce doesn't handle high heat the same way as the tomato sauce).

5 Transfer the dough to the pan and gently form dimples with your fingers.

6 Top the pizza with some of the Buffalo sauce, the provolone, cheddar, green onion, and chicken.

7 Bake for 12–16 minutes or until the crust is deeply golden. Remove from the oven, top with the bleu cheese and another hit of the sauce, cut into squares, and serve.

Brier Hill

Brier Hill pizza, from Youngstown, Ohio, is one of the most Little Italy–inspired in this book. In fact, this style of pizza was thought to have become popular at a Catholic Church, Saint Anthony of Padua. The dough is pretty much Sicilian all day, but the sauce is much closer to a Sunday gravy than anything (and, to be honest, if you used gravy instead of pizza sauce, I wouldn't tell). The flavors rely more on the toppings and sauce than the cheese, so try not to skip those. In fact, you're not going to find a grated mozzarella or provolone on many Brier Hill pizzas; instead, you'll see hard cheeses like Romano. The result is an ultra-savory, fun pie that is packed full of flavor.

BRIER HILL DOUGH

MAKES ONE 14" PIZZA

Ingredients

- **2 cups** (270g) **bread flour**
- **¾ cup** (177mL) **warm water**
- **1 tablespoon** (12g) **sugar**
- **2 teaspoons** (6g) **active dry yeast**
- **¾ teaspoon** (4.5g) **table salt**
- **2 tablespoons** (28g) **vegetable oil**

1 In your stand mixer or a large bowl, gently combine the water, sugar, yeast, and 1 cup of the flour. Once combined, let stand for 5 minutes.

2 Using the hook attachment on low, begin to mix and gently add the remaining flour, salt, and oil.

3 Mix for 5 minutes on medium-low speed, scraping the bowl as needed to keep the dough in the bowl.

4 Transfer the dough to a large, greased bowl and let it rise on the counter for 2–4 hours, punching it down once.

Gluten-Free Alternative

Try making any of the Brier Hill pizzas with one batch of the gluten-free classic pan dough on page 71 to make one 12" pizza. Follow the instructions in the GF pan recipe on page 75.

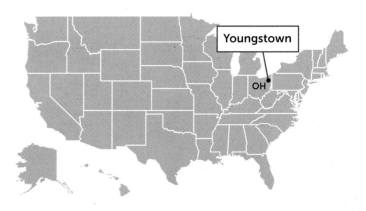

Brier Hill Pepper Pizza

One of my favorite Brier Hill spots is Avalon Downtown Pizzeria in Youngstown, Ohio. Here, they're making pies just like their Italian ancestors, working up dough from scratch every day. Their pies are light yet crunchy, and they do a wonderful job embodying everything a Brier Hill slice can be! Our take on the Brier Hill pie keeps true to the spirit of the original, using only Pecorino Romano and peppers. Here is a prime instance where you want to use imported Pecorino, given how much culinary heavy lifting this cheese does in this pie. Additionally, some spots will cook the sauce with large pieces of green peppers in it, then remove the pieces when topping the pie; feel free to do the same on your pizza to add even more subtle pepper flavor throughout!

Inspiration: With so much Romano, Avalon's Brier Hill is a great representation of the style.

Fluffy, cheesy, and crispy, this slice is ultra-tangy from the Romano and earthy from the pepper notes.

Ingredients

- Brier Hill dough, see page 154
- 2 tablespoons olive oil
- 1 cup crushed tomatoes
- 1 tablespoon Italian seasoning
- 1 teaspoon garlic salt
- 1 pinch red pepper flakes
- 1 bell pepper, sliced and sautéed
- 1 cup shaved Pecorino Romano

Equipment

- 14" lipped pizza pan
- Olive oil for pan

1 Prepare the dough.

2 As the dough rises, combine the oil, crushed tomatoes, Italian seasoning, garlic salt, and red pepper flakes in a small saucepot. Bring to just a simmer and hold for 30 minutes, stirring often. Cool and set aside.

3 Once the dough is risen, preheat the oven to 450°F (230°C). Grease the pan liberally with olive oil.

4 Roll the dough out into a 14" circle, making a small lip all around, then transfer it into the pan.

5 Top the pizza with the sauce, the sautéed peppers, and most of the Pecorino Romano.

6 Bake the pizza for 14–18 minutes or until very brown on all sides. Top with a bit more Pecorino Romano and serve!

Brier Hill Cheese Pizza

Though an authentic Brier Hill pie omits mozzarella, provolone, and the like, many shops do serve more traditional options. Since both the crust and sauce are wonderful flavor contrasts, it tracks that adding softer cheeses also works wonderfully. Here we will make a classic cheese pizza, though this pie tastes anything but simple! Our take will use both provolone and mozzarella, though the addition of some shaved Pecorino Romano adds a nice counterpoint, as well.

The pepper and onion in the sauce add a savory depth to this pizza—envision sopping up a good Sunday gravy with soft bread.

■ **Inspiration:** Avalon's take on a classic cheese pizza tempers the heavy Pecorino Romano with provolone and mozzarella, making the resulting pizza creamier with a more classic feel.

Ingredients

- Brier Hill dough, see page 154
- 2 tablespoons olive oil
- 1 cup crushed tomatoes
- 1 tablespoon Italian seasoning
- 1 teaspoon garlic salt
- ½ green pepper, diced small
- ½ cup diced onion
- 1 pinch red pepper flakes
- 6 ounces provolone, grated
- 6 ounces mozzarella, grated
- ¼ cup shaved Pecorino Romano

Equipment

- 14" lipped pizza pan
- Olive oil for pan

1 Prepare the dough.

2 As the dough rises, combine the oil, crushed tomatoes, Italian seasoning, garlic salt, green pepper, onion, and red pepper flakes in a small saucepot. Bring to just a simmer and hold for 30 minutes, stirring often. Cool and set aside.

3 Once the dough is risen, preheat the oven to 450°F (230°C). Grease the pan liberally with olive oil.

4 Roll the dough out into a 14" circle, making a small lip all around, then transfer it into the pan.

5 Top the pizza with the sauce and the cheeses.

6 Bake the pizza for 12–16 minutes or until very brown on all sides. Remove from the pan and serve!

Omaha

The Omaha pizza was invented somewhere in middle America, and it is truly a unique style. The crust is more like a drop biscuit than a traditional pizza dough and the toppings tend to be more homestyle than Italian (ground beef is a favorite, for example). In total, this pizza is a cross between the Sicilian and a biscuit, but in the best way possible. A rectangular pan is a must here. Don't be surprised if you become hooked on the Omaha pizza.

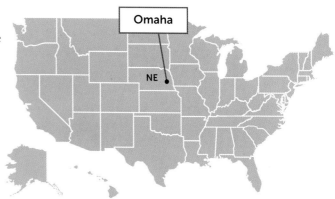

OMAHA DOUGH

MAKES ONE 11" X 17" PIZZA

Ingredients
- 2⅓ cups (280g) **all-purpose flour**
- ¾ cup (180mL) **bottled water, warmed**
- 1 tablespoon (14g) **olive oil**
- 1 teaspoon (4.5g) **baking powder**
- 2 tablespoons (28g) **shortening**
- 1 teaspoon (6g) **table salt**

1 In your stand mixer or a large bowl, combine all the dough ingredients.

2 Mix for 5 minutes on medium-low speed, scraping the bowl as needed to keep the dough in the bowl.

3 Transfer the dough to a large bowl and let it rest on the counter for 1 hour.

OMAHA SAUCE

MAKES ONE 11" X 17" PIZZA

Ingredients
- ⅔ cups **crushed tomatoes**
- 1 teaspoon **Italian seasoning**
- ½ teaspoon **sugar**

1 Combine the crushed tomatoes, Italian seasoning, sugar, and a pinch of salt in a small saucepot.

2 Bring the mixture to just a simmer, then cool until you're ready to cook.

Omaha Hamburger

La Casa Pizzaria, with locations all around Omaha, Nebraska, is synonymous with this style of pie. Founded in 1953, they've been producing high-quality pizzas for decades. Another signature of their pizzas is the use of Romano cheese, which lends a distinct bite to their pies, offering a wonderful contrast against the ultra-savory crust. Their signature pie, the Hamburger, is the perfect place to begin our Omaha pizza journey. In the restaurant, you are given the choice between Romano or mozzarella cheeses—for me, both is the way to go. Our version takes inspiration from the La Casa classic, though we will feature just a light amount of sauce to highlight, but not distract from, the beef and onions on top.

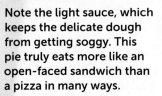

Note the light sauce, which keeps the delicate dough from getting soggy. This pie truly eats more like an open-faced sandwich than a pizza in many ways.

Ingredients

- Omaha dough, see page 157
- Omaha sauce, see page 157
- 1 tablespoon olive oil
- 12 ounces ground beef
- 1 onion, diced and divided
- 2 teaspoons garlic powder
- ½ teaspoon kosher salt
- 8 ounces mozzarella cheese, grated
- 2 ounces Romano, grated

Equipment

- 11" x 17" baking sheet
- Olive oil for greasing
- Large sauté pan

1 Prepare the dough and the sauce.

2 Set a large sauté pan over medium heat. Add in the olive oil then the ground beef and brown it for 5–6 minutes.

3 Add in half of the onion and the garlic powder and kosher salt. Cook for another 2–3 minutes, heavily crumbling the beef, then set it aside to cool.

4 Once the dough is rested, preheat the oven to 425°F (220°C) and lightly grease the baking sheet with olive oil.

5 Roll the dough out into the shape of the baking sheet, using flour as needed to prevent sticking.

6 Lay the dough on the sheet, making a lip against the sides.

7 Top the pizza with sauce, mozzarella, Romano, the remaining onion, and the hamburger mix.

8 Bake the pizza for 16–18 minutes or until very brown on all sides.

Inspiration:
La Casa isn't afraid of loading up their pies—this one has crust-to-crust hamburger covering the Romano and mozzarella. The onions provide a nice sharp counterpoint to the savory meaty flavors, a welcome contrast to cut through the richness.

Omaha Supreme

Another classic pie at La Casa is the Carne Classico, which is a meat lover's dream. This pie goes hard, and provides one savory bite after another, featuring pepperoni, spicy sausage, and prosciutto and either Romano or mozzarella cheeses. Let's build our own take on a supreme pizza with our Omaha dough, and since I can't decide between Romano or mozzarella, I'll choose both.

I love crumbling the sausage like the old-school fast food pizza places—it just hits different.

■ **Inspiration:** La Casa's pie is an overload of meaty goodness in which the trio of pepperoni, spicy sausage, and prosciutto brings an umami bomb of flavor.

Ingredients
- Omaha dough, see page 157
- Omaha sauce, see page 157
- 4 ounces hot Italian sausage, cooked and crumbled
- 8 ounces mozzarella cheese, grated
- 2 ounces Romano, grated
- 4 ounces pepperoni
- ½ cup diced bell peppers
- ¼ cup diced white onion

Equipment
- 11" x 17" baking sheet
- Olive oil for greasing

1 Prepare the dough and the sauce.

2 Once the dough is rested, preheat the oven to 425°F (220°C) and lightly grease the baking sheet with olive oil.

3 Roll the dough out into the shape of the baking sheet, using flour as needed to prevent sticking.

4 Lay the dough on the sheet, making a lip against the sides.

5 Top the pizza with sauce, mozzarella, Romano, sausage, pepperoni, bell pepper, and onion.

6 Bake the pizza for 16–18 minutes or until very brown on all sides.

Old Forge

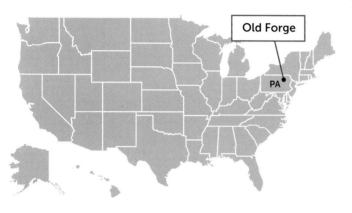

Old Forge

PA

OLD FORGE DOUGH

MAKES ONE 11" X 17" PIZZA

Ingredients

- **1½ cups** (202g) **bread flour**
- **½ cup** (118ml) **bottled water**
- **1 teaspoon** (4g) **sugar**
- **1 tablespoon** (14g) **butter**
- **¾ teaspoon** (4.5g) **table salt**
- **1 teaspoon** (3g) **instant yeast**

1 In the work bowl of your stand mixer, add the bread flour, water, sugar, butter, salt, and yeast in that order.

2 Using the hook attachment, work the ingredients for 3 minutes on low speed or until combined.

3 Let rest for 10 minutes, then work again for another 5 minutes on low speed.

4 Remove the dough from the bowl and form it into a ball.

5 Place the dough ball into a large, greased bowl. Cover it and let it rise on the counter for 8 hours, punching it down twice after every 2–3 hours.

According to some purists, the pizza capital of the world is . . . Old Forge, Pennsylvania. The Old Forge pizza makes its home near Scranton (cue *The Office* theme), and it has some rules. First, the pizza is a tray, not a pie, and it's served in cuts, not slices. Two styles exist—red, a more familiar pizza, and white, which is closer to a pizza puff. As far as flavor goes, the Old Forge is akin to the grandma pie (in the Sicilian family, rectangular, and crisp and bready) with a Sunday gravy–style sauce (heavy on the onion, with a long simmer). The cheese is usually a blend of white cheddar, American, and mozzarella. Some Old Forge pizzas will feature thinly sliced onions, which seem to melt onto the pie. The resulting tray is delightfully familiar, yet highly unusual and interesting. Another fun aspect of the Old Forge is the parbake (partially bake), which is typical of many in the region. This has advantages for the home cook, allowing for more prep ahead of time.

Classic Old Forge

For this recipe, we will take a cheesy page from the Detroit-style playbook to enhance the flavor of this regional classic.

Ingredients

- Old Forge dough, see page 161
- 2 tablespoons olive oil
- 2 cloves garlic, crushed
- ¼ cup onion, minced
- 1 cup crushed tomatoes
- 1 tablespoon Italian seasoning
- 1 pinch red pepper flakes
- 6 ounces mozzarella cheese, grated
- 3 ounces white cheddar cheese, grated
- ¼ cup grated Pecorino Romano

Equipment

- 11" x 17" baking sheet with a lip
- Shortening
- Cooling rack

1 Prepare the dough.

2 Place the olive oil in a saucepot over medium heat. Once warm, add the garlic and cook for 1 minute, stirring the entire time. Add in the diced onion and cook for 1 more minute.

3 Add the tomatoes, then season with the Italian seasoning, red pepper flakes, and a pinch of salt. Cook on low heat for 20 minutes. Keep cool until ready to use.

4 Once the dough has risen, place it onto a lightly floured work surface and press it into a rough rectangle, about the size of the pan, then let it rest for 20 minutes.

5 Preheat the oven to 475°F (245°C) and place a rack in the lower third of the oven. Grease the pan with shortening.

6 Once the dough has rested, transfer it to the greased pan. Form a lip against the sides and press the dough into the corners.

7 Cover the dough and let it rest for another 30 minutes, then uncover and parbake (partially bake) it for 5 minutes.

8 Once parbaked, carefully remove the dough from the pan and let it cool on the cooling rack for at least 15 minutes.

9 Top the pizza with the sauce and cheeses. Bake for another 8–10 minutes or until the crust is brown.

10 Remove the cooked pizza from the oven and let it cool for 5 minutes. Once cool, transfer it to a cutting board, cut it into squares, serve, and enjoy.

> Once you've parbaked the dough, you don't have to use it right away—you can also chill it to use later (for up to three days)!

This is just a really nice tray of pizza, and a favorite of my kids. It's straightforward but never basic, unfussy and familiar.

Old Forge White Pizza

There is a pizza institution in downtown Old Forge, Pennsylvania, that has been making trays since 1967: Revello's Pizza. Currently run by Pat Revello, son of the founders, their Old Forge slices are world famous, and for good reason. At Revello's, their classic tomato-based Red trays are rivaled only by their White, a wonderful cheesy creation. The White Old Forge is akin to a pizza puff, and while we will use the same dough, the similarities end there. The Old Forge white lives between a pastry and pizza; think of it as almost a Sicilian cheese-filled pastry.

Ingredients

- 2 batches Old Forge dough, see page 161
- 1 tablespoon olive oil
- 6 ounces Monterey Jack cheese, grated
- 6 ounces provolone cheese, grated
- 3 ounces fontina cheese, grated
- 1 teaspoon dried oregano
- 3 cloves garlic, crushed
- ¼ cup grated Parmesan
- ½ teaspoon garlic powder
- ½ teaspoon black pepper

Equipment

- 11" x 17" baking sheet with a lip
- Shortening

1 Prepare the dough.

2 Once the dough has risen, divide it into two equal balls and place both onto a lightly floured work surface. Work each ball into a rectangle about the size of the pan.

3 Preheat the oven to 450°F (230°C) and grease the pan with shortening.

4 Transfer one of the dough rectangles to the greased pan. Brush the dough with the olive oil, then top it with the cheeses, oregano, and garlic.

5 Gently place the remaining dough on top and crimp closed on all sides. Take your time and be gentle; the dough should just meet when stretched.

6 Make three small slits in the top for steam to escape, then top with the grated Parmesan, garlic powder, and black pepper.

7 Bake for 20–24 minutes or until nicely browned. Cool, cut into squares, and serve.

This tray is cheese overload, and the dough is the perfect thickness to hold and complement the gooey center.

Inspiration:
Trays and trays of goodness, Revello's white pizza is a cross between a grilled cheese, a calzone, and a quesadilla, of all things. The texture of the cheese layer is oozy perfection.

Ohio Valley

Ohio Valley pizza is certainly one of the most distinctive variants we will cover in this book. This one is closer to a Lunchables® than a traditional pizza, but oddly in the best way possible. The crust is sweet and crisp, while everything else is cold. The dough is blind baked hot with just enough sauce to keep it from burning, then finished with cold cheese and toppings. The first bake with the sauce caramelizes the tomatoes, playing into the dichotomy of sweet versus savory and hot versus cold. It's a bit more like an open-faced sandwich than a pizza (especially given the extremely low-hydration dough), but it's strangely addicting, nonetheless. Don't sleep on this pizza, which makes wonderful picnic fare or an excellent make-ahead pizza.

Ohio Valley

OHIO VALLEY DOUGH

MAKES ONE 16" X 16" OR 13" X 18" PIZZA

Ingredients
- 3¼ cups (420g) **bread flour**
- 1 cup (237ml) **filtered water**
- 1 tablespoon (12g) **sugar**
- 1 teaspoon (3g) **active dry yeast**
- 1½ teaspoons (9g) **table salt**

1 In your stand mixer or large bowl, combine the water, sugar, yeast, and 1 cup of flour. Gently combine and let stand for 3 minutes.

2 Following the rest period, begin to mix using the hook attachment on low. Gently pour in the remaining flour and salt, then mix for 5 minutes on medium-low speed (scraping the bowl as needed to keep the dough in the bowl).

3 Once mixed, form the dough into a ball and cover it with a clean towel and let it rise on the counter for 4 hours, punching it down every hour.

OHIO VALLEY SAUCE

MAKES ONE 16" X 16" OR 13" X 18" PIZZA

Ingredients
- 2 cups **crushed tomatoes**
- 2 cloves **garlic**
- ⅓ cup **diced onion**
- ¼ cup **diced green pepper**
- 1 teaspoon **dried Italian herbs**
- 3 tablespoons **olive oil**
- ½ teaspoon **salt**

1 Combine the crushed tomatoes, garlic, onion, green pepper, dried herbs, olive oil, and salt in a slow cooker set on high.

2 Let the mixture cook on low for 4 hours, stirring occasionally.

Ohio Valley Pizza

When the pizzeria is literally named after the style of pizza, you know you are in the right place. So, when I say that Ohio Valley Pizza Co. in Newell, West Virginia, is my go-to for this style of pie, you know it's legit. Many Ohio Valley pizza enthusiasts know that DiCarlo's was the originator of this style, so wisely, the owners of Ohio Valley Pizza Co., Amy and Dave Byers, reached out to them to work out the ins and outs of this pie. The result? A wonderful, authentic, and inspired pizza that holds up to any and all other styles in this book. Note that the pizzas at Ohio Valley Pizza Co. are 16" x 16" (if you don't have a pan this size, a 13" x 18" pan will do). Also, the exact dough and sauce recipes are a trade secret, so what we will be making is an "average" of the flavors in the region. If you want the real Ohio Valley Pizza Co. version, plan a stop! Until then, let's make an at-home approximation of this fabulous Midwestern pie.

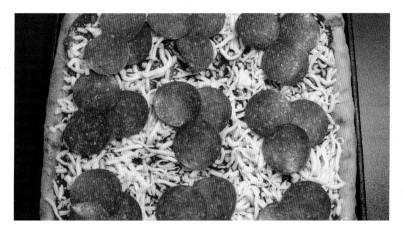

These slices taste almost like a cold-cut sandwich, where the cold cheese and pepperoni are in perfect contrast to the crust and tomatoes.

■ **Inspiration:** Hot pizza, cold cheese—the play on temperatures makes Ohio Valley Pizza Co.'s pizza extremely interesting, as the cheese flavor is a bit more prominent on the palate.

Ingredients
- Ohio Valley dough, see page 166
- Ohio Valley sauce, see page 166
- 8 ounces mozzarella, shredded
- 6 ounces provolone, shredded
- 3 ounces thinly sliced pepperoni

Equipment
- 16" x 16" or 13" x 18" baking sheet

1 Prepare the dough and the sauce.

2 Once the dough has risen, preheat the oven to 450°F (230°C).

3 Roll the dough out into the shape of the baking sheet, using flour as needed to prevent sticking.

4 Lay the dough on the sheet, pressing it into the sides to create a lip.

5 Liberally dock the dough (poke holes into it to let steam release during baking) with a fork, then top it with 1 cup of the sauce.

6 Bake for 7–8 minutes, then remove the pizza from the oven.

7 Top the pizza with another thin layer of sauce (about ¼ cup) and 1 ounce of the mozzarella cheese.

8 Bake for another 6–8 minutes until the crust is set and golden, then remove the pizza from the oven and let it cool for 3–4 minutes.

9 Top the pizza with the remaining cold cheese and the pepperoni. Let sit for another 3–4 minutes, then cut the pizza into squares and serve alongside the remaining sauce for dipping.

Ohio Valley Pizza "Molten"

While the classic Ohio Valley pizza is the hot crust/cold cheese combo, there is one other variant that warrants highlighting. Called "molten," this version looks like a traditional pizza, with melted cheese and everything. While I understand it is not frequently ordered, I really enjoy this slice; the crisp crust makes a pizza that is texturally inviting. The ingredients are actually identical to the other version, but the method used makes it into a completely different creation.

Ingredients

- Ohio Valley dough, see page 166
- Ohio Valley sauce, see page 166
- 8 ounces mozzarella, shredded
- 6 ounces provolone, shredded
- 3 ounces thinly sliced pepperoni

Equipment

- 11" x 17" baking sheet
- Olive oil for greasing

1 Prepare the dough and the sauce.

2 Once the dough has risen, preheat the oven to 450°F (**230°C**) and set your rack in the lower third of your oven. Grease the baking sheet with the olive oil.

3 Roll the dough out into the shape of the baking sheet, using flour as needed to prevent sticking.

4 Lay the dough on the sheet, pressing it into the sides to create a lip.

5 Liberally dock the dough (poke holes into it to let steam release during baking) with a fork, then top it with 1 cup of the sauce.

6 Bake for 7 minutes, then remove the pizza from the oven and let it cool for 15 minutes on the counter.

7 Top the pizza with another thin layer of sauce (about ¼ cup), the cheese, and the pepperoni.

8 Bake for another 6–8 minutes until the crust is set and golden and the cheese is just melted. Cut the pizza into squares and serve.

> After the first bake, you can also hold the crust in the refrigerator overnight and continue cooking the next day.

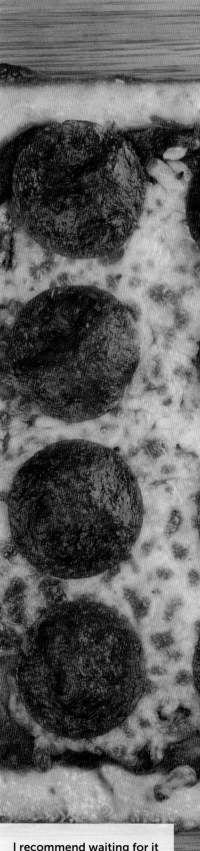

I recommend waiting for it to not be "molten" before eating, but that's your call.

Inspiration:
This isn't the most popular pizza in the region, but when high-quality ingredients are used like they are in Ohio Valley Pizza Co.'s pie, the versatility shines. This is a pleasing molten slice that rivals any in this book.

Cleveland

Cleveland

OH

The Cleveland or Ohio-style pizza is awfully controversial for a pizza coming from the Buckeye state. The dough, a cross between the Chicago tavern and grandma pie, is bready and a bit flaky due to the butter used. The result is a hybrid pan/Sicilian sort of slice, which is a balance of a crisp crust and spongy dough. Another must is the thick, hand-cut pepperoni, which just seems to hit different on this style.

CLEVELAND DOUGH

MAKES ONE 14" PIZZA

Ingredients

- 2 cups (270g) **bread flour**
- ¾ cup (177ml) **warm water**
- 1 tablespoon (12g) **sugar**
- 2 teaspoons (6g) **instant yeast**
- ¾ teaspoon (4.5g) **table salt**
- 2 tablespoons (28g) **melted butter**

1 In your stand mixer or large bowl, combine the water, sugar, yeast, and 1 cup of flour. Gently combine and let stand for 5 minutes.

2 Following the rest period, begin to mix using the hook attachment on low. Gently pour in the remaining flour, salt, and butter. Mix for 5 minutes on medium-low speed (scraping the bowl as needed to keep the dough in the bowl).

3 Transfer the dough to a large, greased bowl and let it rise on the counter for 4 hours, punching it down once. Once the first rise is complete, store it in the fridge overnight.

4 Remove the dough from refrigerator 3 hours before pizza cooking time.

CLEVELAND SAUCE

MAKES ONE 14" PIZZA

Ingredients

- 2 tablespoons olive oil
- ¾ cup crushed tomatoes
- 1 tablespoon Italian seasoning
- 1 teaspoon garlic salt
- 1 pinch red pepper flakes

1 Combine the oil, crushed tomatoes, Italian seasoning, garlic salt, and red pepper flakes in a small saucepot.

2 Bring the mixture to just a simmer. Keep cool until you're ready to cook.

GARLIC BUTTER

MAKES ONE 14" PIZZA

Ingredients

- 3 tablespoons melted butter
- 2 cloves of garlic, crushed

1 Warm the butter in a small saucepot over low heat.

2 Add the garlic and steep for 15 minutes; be sure not to get color on the garlic. Keep cool until you're ready to cook.

Cleveland Cheese with Garlic Butter

Geraci's Restaurant, with five locations in and around Cleveland, embodies the heart of Cleveland-style pizza. Founded in 1956 by Michael and Frances Geraci, this spot has been a Cleveland tradition for 67 years. Establishing their roots in University Heights, the family-friendly restaurant has been proudly serving their traditional Italian entrées and award-winning pizza for generations. Heavily lauded, Geraci's is one of the ultimate Cleveland-style pizza spots. We will start with a classic cheese pie; feel free to serve with hot honey, which is a familiar add-on at Geraci's, along with my take on their Bucky Butter, a garlic butter you never knew you needed in your life until this moment.

The garlic butter on this pizza is inspired by the favorite dipping sauce at Geraci's, adding a wonderful flavor bomb to this already incredible pie.

■ **Inspiration:** That cheese edge on the crust makes Geraci's pizza—it's a crunchy cheese rim that is *everything*, especially against the melty provolone.

Ingredients

- Cleveland dough, see page 170
- Cleveland sauce, see page 171
- Garlic butter, see page 171
- 8 ounces provolone, shredded
- ¼ cup grated Parmesan

Equipment

- 14" pizza pan
- Shortening

1 Sometime before pizza day, prepare the sauce and the garlic butter.

2 Remove the dough from the fridge 3 hours before cooking time.

3 Once the dough is back to room temperature, preheat the oven to 450°F (230°C). Grease the pizza pan with shortening.

4 Roll the dough out into a 14" circle, using flour as needed to prevent sticking. Make a gentle lip around the outside edge. Lay the dough on the greased pizza pan.

5 Top the pizza with the sauce, provolone, and Parmesan.

6 Bake for 16–20 minutes or until brown on all sides. Swirl on the garlic butter, cut, and enjoy!

Cleveland Pepperoni

It is wild that adding one simple ingredient can transform an entire pizza, but once you've experienced thick, hand-cut pepperoni, you'll understand why. Instead of pre-sliced, opt for an entire pepperoni link. Chill it thoroughly and hand slice it to ¼" thick. No need for the garlic butter here; the pepperoni provides all of the flavor we need and then some. If you want to lean out this pie just a hair, gently sweat the pepperoni in a pan over low heat for 4–5 minutes to render out a bit of the pepperoni grease. (Also, if you're interested more in flavor experimentation than lightness, try swapping this pepperoni grease in for the olive oil in the sauce—you're in for a treat!) In our version, we go a little thicker with the crust as a changeup to the previous recipe, showcasing the range this particular style has.

This pie showcases a thicker crust that works well against the thick pepperoni.

Inspiration: All that crispy pepperoni, with the pepperoni grease seeping throughout the pizza, is truly remarkable. The result is a spicy, tangy flavor that bakes directly into Geraci's pizza.

Ingredients

- Cleveland dough, see page 170
- Cleveland sauce, see page 171
- 8 ounces provolone, shredded
- ¼ cup grated Parmesan
- 5 ounces pepperoni, hand-cut

Equipment

- 14" pizza pan

1 Sometime before pizza day, prepare the sauce.

2 Remove the dough from the fridge 3 hours before cooking time.

3 Once the dough is back to room temperature, preheat the oven to 450°F (230°C). Grease the pizza pan with shortening.

4 Roll the dough out into a 14" circle, using flour as needed to prevent sticking. Make a gentle lip around the outside edge. Lay the dough on the pizza pan.

5 Top the pizza with the sauce, provolone, Parmesan, and pepperoni.

6 Bake for 16–20 minutes or until brown on all sides. Once cooked, cut and enjoy!

Thin
Style

Thin-crust pizza is defined by its delicate, crisp base, which provides the ideal foundation for toppings and flavors. With roots in Italy and perfected across various American regions, thin-crust pizza has become the go-to style for a crispy, crunchy experience that allows toppings to shine without overwhelming the crust. From the ultra-crispy tavern-style pies of the Midwest to the boardwalk styles in New Jersey, each region brings its own twist to the thin-crust tradition. This style often involves rolling out the dough very thin and cooking it at high temperatures for a brief time, resulting in a light, crackling bite.

Thin-crust pizza, from the Chicago tavern to the St. Louis and everything in between, is the perfect example of how contrasting textures make for amazing pizza.

Chicago Tavern

Chicago tavern-style (or pub) pizza is the pizza that most Chicagoans actually eat when they eat pizza. As thin and crisp as possible, with more toppings than is likely prudent, this pizza pairs perfectly with a cold beer and Big Ten football. The crust is cracker-thin, but unlike some other thin pizzas, it still holds texture and maintains a familiar flavor. The sauce is on the sweeter side, pairing nicely with both the charred crust and the savory cheese. There is also a trick to the tavern pie—by leaving it formed in the fridge overnight, we "cure" the dough, making for an extremely crisp crust. Pro tip: Always cut it into squares (the party cut), so you can reserve the subsequent corner triangles for the chef.

CHICAGO TAVERN DOUGH

MAKES TWO 12" TO 14" PIZZAS

Ingredients

- 2½ cups (337g) **bread flour**
- ¾ cup (177mL) **warm water**
- 2 teaspoons (8g) **sugar**
- 1 teaspoon (3g) **active dry yeast**
- 1½ teaspoons (9g) **salt**
- 2 tablespoons (28g) **vegetable oil**

Equipment

- 2 tablespoons cornmeal
- Two 14" pizza pans

1 In your stand mixer or large bowl, gently combine the water, sugar, yeast, and 1 cup of flour. Let stand for 3 minutes.

2 Following the rest period, mix on low with the hook attachment.

3 Gently pour in the remaining flour, the salt, and oil. Mix for 5 minutes on medium-low speed. The dough will be a little dry—that's normal.

4 Transfer the dough to a large, greased bowl, cover it, and let it rise on the counter for 4 hours, punching it down once.

5 Once the dough has risen, divide it into two balls and roll each out into 12" to 14" circles, as thin as you can make them. Do not worry too much about the shape at this point.

6 Sprinkle the cornmeal into your pizza pans, lay in the dough, then let them both sit, uncovered, in the refrigerator overnight.

7 Remove the pizza dough from the fridge and cut and shape as needed when you preheat the oven.

Gluten-Free Alternative

Gluten-free thin crusts can be very successful. I use Caputo Fioreglut Gluten Free Flour, because I find it to be the closest to traditional flour and the easiest to work with. Feel free to use your favorite GF flour, just note that some trial and error will be needed. See page 182 for a full recipe using the gluten-free thin dough.

GLUTEN-FREE THIN DOUGH

MAKES TWO 10" PIZZAS

Ingredients
- 2 cups (180g) Caputo Fioreglut Gluten Free Flour
- ½ cup plus 1 tablespoon (135g) water
- 1 tablespoon (15g) extra-virgin olive oil
- ¾ teaspoon (4.5g) salt
- ⅛ teaspoon (0.5g) instant yeast

1 In the work bowl of your stand mixer, combine the water, yeast, and olive oil.

2 Slowly add in the flour and salt and work on low using the hook attachment for 5–10 minutes.

3 Cover and let the dough rise for 1–2 hours.

4 When the dough has about doubled, divide it in half and let it proof in the fridge for another 3–4 hours.

CHICAGO TAVERN SAUCE

MAKES TWO 12" TO 14" PIZZAS

Ingredients
- 3 tablespoons olive oil
- ¼ cup tomato paste
- 1 cup crushed tomatoes
- 2 teaspoons Italian seasoning

1 Combine the olive oil, tomato paste, crushed tomatoes, a pinch of salt, and Italian seasoning in a small saucepot.

2 Bring the mixture to just a simmer, then whisk to thoroughly incorporate the tomato paste and cook for 10 minutes on low.

3 Cool and set aside in the refrigerator for future use.

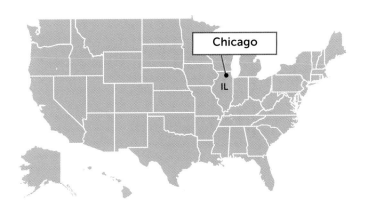

Chicago

IL

Chicago Tavern Pizza

We begin our tavern pizza journey with a cheese pie, which works so amazingly well. The cheese layer is thicker than the dough, but the crisp crust holds up perfectly, creating an ultra-cheesy bite in every square. The curing of the dough is a brilliantly simple method that creates a perfect tavern pie. Feel free to finish this pizza with some dried oregano or red pepper flakes to get that true tavern feel.

Inspiration: This is a cheese tavern-style pie by John Carruthers, a man who would be on the Mount Rushmore of Chicago tavern pies.

Ingredients
- Chicago tavern dough, see page 176
- Chicago tavern sauce, see page 177
- 12 ounces mozzarella cheese, grated
- ¼ cup grated Parmesan

Equipment
- 2 tablespoons cornmeal, see page 176
- Two 14" pizza pans, see page 176

1 Sometime before pizza day, prepare the sauce.

2 Preheat the oven to 450°F (230°C). Remove the two pizzas from the fridge and cut and shape each as needed into rounds.

3 Top each pizza with half of the sauce and mozzarella. Finish each with a heavy sprinkle of Parmesan. Make sure to add sauce to the very edge of each pizza and add cheese out very close to the edge.

4 Bake for 12–14 minutes or until very brown on all sides. Cut each into 2" squares and serve as soon as they're cool enough that you won't burn the roof of your mouth.

G&Jim

Tavern-style pizza is very near and dear to my heart. Having lived above a pizzeria during some of my time in Chicago, I became very fond of this style of pizza as served at one of my favorite places in the world, Flo & Santos. This pizzeria features both Chicago tavern pizza as well as Polish favorites like pierogies, and I've never had a bad time here. This is the place I took my wife on the night we got engaged, their back room hosted our wedding rehearsal dinner, and they've hosted dozens of our memories in between. After many, many rounds of trial and error with the owners, my wife and I found our perfect pizza combo, a pie we call the G&Jim. The thick-cut pepperoni adds the perfect flavor and a textural counterpoint to the crisp crust, contrasting against the tangy goat cheese and sweet sun-dried tomatoes.

This topping combo took many (delicious) years to perfect—the tangy goat cheese, the sweetness from the sun-dried tomatoes, and the red onion to keep everything in balance. My wife helped make the pie shown here, bringing our pizza journey full circle.

Ingredients

- Chicago tavern dough, see page 176
- Chicago tavern sauce, see page 177
- ⅓ cup sliced red onion
- ⅓ cup sun-dried tomatoes
- 8 ounces mozzarella cheese, grated
- 3 ounces goat cheese
- 4 ounces pepperoni, thick-cut

Equipment

- 2 tablespoons cornmeal, see page 176
- Two 14" pizza pans, see page 176

1 Sometime before pizza day, prepare the sauce.

2 Preheat the oven to 450°F (230°C). Remove the two pizzas from the fridge and cut and shape each as needed into rounds.

3 Top each pizza with half of the sauce, red onions, sun-dried tomatoes, mozzarella, goat cheese, and pepperoni. Make sure to add sauce to the very edge of each pizza.

4 Bake for 12–14 minutes or until very brown on all sides. Cut each into 2" squares and serve.

Italian Beef Tavern Pizza

Flo & Santos does a wonderful job of weaving local favorites into their pies, and this is just one perfect example. The Marco is a mashup of tavern pizza and a Chicago Italian beef. This is truly the best of both worlds, and to be completely honest, I add giardiniera (a spicy, fermented pepper mixture that is in fact the world's finest food) to most pizzas I eat. If Italian beef isn't something you can readily find, I suggest swapping it for the same amount of cooked hot Italian sausage, which is also an absolute classic!

Don't be afraid to add both hot Italian sausage and Italian beef (those in the know call that The Combo).

Inspiration: Two Chicago classics in one—hats off to Flo & Santos. The giardiniera adds a fermented spice that cannot be replicated with anything else, cutting through the rich beef and cheese.

Ingredients

- Chicago tavern dough, see page 176
- Chicago tavern sauce, see page 176
- 8 ounces mozzarella cheese, grated
- 4 ounces cooked Italian beef or shaved steak
- ¼ cup grated Parmesan
- ½ cup Chicago-style giardiniera

Equipment

- 2 tablespoons cornmeal, see page 176
- Two 14" pizza pans, see page 176

1 Sometime before pizza day, prepare the sauce.

2 Preheat the oven to 450°F (230°C). Remove the two pizzas from the fridge and cut and shape each as needed into rounds.

3 Top each pizza with half of the sauce, mozzarella, Italian beef, and Parmesan.

4 Bake for 10 minutes. Remove the pizzas from the oven, top each with half the giardiniera, and cook for another 2–4 minutes. Cut each into 2" squares and serve.

Polish Tavern Pizza

Want to go even fuller Chicago? Try this combo, based on the famous version at Flo & Santos. I know what you're thinking, but this is another one that would be on the Mount Rushmore of pizzas. Trust me.

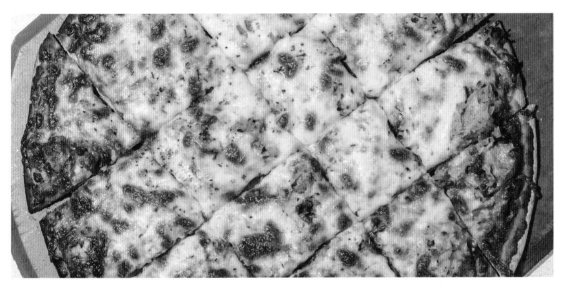

■■■ **Inspiration:** This Flo & Santos classic, a culinary fusion of Polish and Italian, absolutely works. The sauerkraut adds a tartness that allows for the savory and smoky kielbasa and bacon to shine.

Ingredients

- Chicago tavern dough, see page 176
- Chicago tavern sauce, see page 177
- 8 ounces mozzarella cheese, grated
- ¼ cup cooked and crumbled bacon
- 4 ounces cooked kielbasa, sliced thin
- ⅓ cup sauerkraut

Equipment

- 2 tablespoons cornmeal, see page 176
- Two 14" pizza pans, see page 176

1 Sometime before pizza day, prepare the sauce.

2 Preheat the oven to 450°F (230°C). Remove the two pizzas from the fridge and cut and shape each as needed into rounds.

3 Top each pizza with half of the sauce, mozzarella, bacon, and kielbasa.

4 Bake for 10 minutes. Remove the pizzas from the oven, top each with half the sauerkraut, and cook for another 2–4 minutes. Cut each into 2" squares and enjoy one of the best foods you'll ever eat.

GF Thin

Gluten-free dough works wonderfully for thin-crust pies. The particular makeup of the flour lends itself to very crisp crusts that don't get soggy or limp easily. Truth be told, I almost prefer a GF flour when making a standard thin-crust pie.

This crust gets amazingly crisp and tastes just like a tavern-style pizza.

Ingredients

- Gluten-free thin dough, see page 177
- ½ cup passata or tomato puree
- 4 ounces fresh mozzarella, sliced into ½" pieces and drained
- 3 tablespoons extra-virgin olive oil
- 8–10 basil leaves

Equipment

- Two 12" pizza pans
- Olive oil for greasing

1 Prepare the dough.

2 Once the dough has proofed, preheat the oven to 475°F (245°C) and move a rack to the lower third of the oven. Lightly oil each pizza pan.

3 Roll each pizza out into a 10" to 12" circle and transfer each to a pizza pan.

4 Top each pizza with half of the passata and mozzarella, leaving a ½" border of crust all around the outside.

5 Bake for 14–16 minutes or until the pizzas are golden around the edges. Transfer to a cutting board, garnish with the basil and olive oil, cut into slices, and devour.

St. Louis

This recipe was the last I wrote for the book because it was the hardest to nail. The cheese classically used in St. Louis-style pizza is Provel®, a processed cheese akin to a firm white nacho cheese. The crust is barely leavened and is closer to a cracker than a pizza dough. This unique pizza resembles something more like a tostada than a pizza (not that that's a bad thing!).

ST. LOUIS-STYLE DOUGH

MAKES TWO 12" PIZZAS

Ingredients

- 1 ¾ cups (240g) **bread flour**
- ½ cup (118mL) **water**
- 1 teaspoon (5g) **baking powder**
- 1 teaspoon (6g) **table salt**
- 1 teaspoon (4g) **sugar**
- 2 tablespoons (28g) **vegetable oil**

1 In your stand mixer or large bowl, combine the water, sugar, baking powder, salt, sugar, and oil.

2 Using the hook attachment or your hands, mix on low for 2–3 minutes or until the dough comes together. Let it rest or 15 minutes.

Gluten-Free Alternative

Gluten-free? Try making any of the St. Louis pizzas with one batch of the gluten-free thin dough on page 177. Follow the instructions in the GF thin recipe on page 182.

ST. LOUIS SAUCE

MAKES TWO 12" PIZZAS

Ingredients

- ⅔ cup **crushed tomatoes**
- 2 tablespoons **sugar**
- ½ teaspoon **salt**
- 1 teaspoon **dried Italian herbs**

1 Combine the crushed tomatoes, sugar, salt, and Italian herbs, no cooking needed.

2 Set aside for future use.

St. Louis Cheese

This recipe follows the standard St. Louis style with the obvious exception of using our own cheese blend (because you likely won't be able to source Provel). This makes for a very nice pie, but if you feel inspired and are able to find it, swap out the cheeses for Provel and proceed as directed!

The tavern cut is a must for the extremely thin St. Louis pie (so you can eat more).

Ingredients
- St. Louis-style dough, see page 183
- St. Louis sauce, see page 183
- ¾ cup white cheddar cheese, grated
- ¾ cup provolone cheese, grated
- ½ cup fontina cheese, grated

Equipment
- Parchment paper
- Nonstick spray
- Two 12" pizza pans

1 Prepare the dough.

2 As the dough rests, prepare the sauce and combine all the grated cheeses.

3 Preheat the oven to 425°F (220°C). Spray a piece of parchment paper with the nonstick spray.

4 Divide the dough ball in half and place the sprayed parchment paper on top of one half and roll it out as thin as possible. Aim for the thickness of two quarters stacked and 12" around. Repeat with the other half of the dough.

5 Place each crust on a pizza pan and top each with half of the sauce and the cheese blend. Push the sauce and cheese out to the edge.

6 Bake for 10–12 minutes or until the crust begins to brown (this crust goes from brown to black quickly, so don't let it go too long). Cut into squares and enjoy!

Tortilla Pizza

Short on time? Use a 12" flour tortilla for the crust, which I'm not saying is actually better, but it's sure as heck not worse, especially given the utter ease of this option. Think of this as the ultimate midnight snack or emergency dinner. If there is one trick to this style, it is moisture control. The use of oil on both sides of the tortilla will prevent a soggy bottom, which no one needs in their life.

This might not be the fanciest pie in this book, but sometimes you just need a pizza on zero minutes' notice!

Ingredients
- Two 12" flour tortillas
- St. Louis sauce, see page 183
- 1 tablespoon olive oil
- 2 ounces white cheddar cheese, grated
- 2 ounces provolone cheese, grated
- 2 ounces fontina cheese, grated

Equipment
- Nonstick spray
- Two 12" pizza pans

1 Prepare the sauce and combine all the grated cheeses.

2 Preheat the oven to 425°F (220°C). Spray each pan with the nonstick spray.

3 Brush each tortilla on both sides with olive oil and place one tortilla on each pan.

4 Top each tortilla with half of the sauce and the cheese blend. Push the sauce and cheese out to the edge.

5 Bake for 5–6 minutes or until the tortillas begin to brown. Cut into squares and enjoy!

Sausage, Pepper, and Tomato St. Louis Pizza

For this one, I went deep down the rabbit hole and found a few pizza masters who maintain the essence of the St. Louis style while crafting around the parts that some may find less desirable. A great place to start is the restaurant that very likely invented the style, Monte Bello Pizzeria in St. Louis, Missouri. Founded in 1950, it is the oldest St. Louis-style pizzeria around. Also extremely notable is that Monte Bello doesn't use Provel (and many say Provel was actually designed around their cheese blend, not the other way around). My favorite pizza at Monte Bello is "The Sandy," a pie featuring double homemade Italian sausage, roasted tomatoes, and garlic. A bold pie, but a winner in my book. Here, we're borrowing the concept of the sausage and tomatoes, though nestling the tomatoes under the cheese to add to the texture of this pie. Be sure to find the hottest Italian sausage around; you won't regret it here. Our version also does not use Provel and uses a different mix of cheeses than Monte Bello uses but it's a nice proxy to the general St. Louis style. I also throw on some peppers, which highlights the other flavors nicely.

Ingredients

- St. Louis-style dough, see page 183
- St. Louis sauce, see page 183
- 1 tablespoon olive oil
- 1 Roma tomato, sliced thin
- ¾ cup white cheddar cheese, grated
- ¾ cup provolone cheese, grated
- ¾ cup fontina cheese, grated
- 8 ounces hot Italian sausage, cooked and crumbled
- ½ bell pepper, thinly sliced

Equipment

- Parchment paper
- Nonstick spray
- Two 12" pizza pans

1 Prepare the dough.

2 As the dough rests, prepare the sauce and combine all the grated cheeses.

3 Preheat the oven to 425°F (220°C). Spray a piece of parchment paper with the nonstick spray.

4 Divide the dough ball in half and place the sprayed parchment paper on top of one half and roll it out as thin as possible. Aim for the thickness of two quarters stacked and 12" around. Repeat with the other half of the dough.

5 Place each crust on a pizza pan and top each with half of the sauce, tomatoes, cheeses, sausage, and peppers. Push the sauce and cheese out to the edge.

6 Bake for 10–14 minutes or until the crust begins to brown. Cut into squares and enjoy!

Nestling the tomatoes under the cheese helps add a different textural component to this pie. There's a lot of love in each square.

■ *Inspiration:*
This is a solid pie from Monte Bello's, where the blend of cheeses is the star, lending to a creamy, salty bite that is truly unique.

Toasted Ravioli Pizza

There is one other thing about St. Louis cuisine that I enjoy as much as the pizza—toasted ravioli, a ravioli that is breaded and fried à la mozzarella stick. Mashed up with a St. Louis pizza, you create something absolutely unforgettable.

The swirl on this rich pie is melted ricotta cheese.

Ingredients

- St. Louis-style dough, see page 183
- St. Louis sauce, see page 183
- 3 ounces white cheddar cheese, grated
- 3 ounces provolone cheese, grated
- ½ cup ricotta cheese
- 2 tablespoons Italian breadcrumbs

Equipment

- Parchment paper
- Nonstick spray
- Two 12" pizza pans

1 Prepare the dough.

2 As the dough rests, prepare the sauce and combine the cheddar and provolone.

3 Preheat the oven to 425°F (220°C). Spray a piece of parchment paper with the nonstick spray.

4 Divide the dough ball in half and place the sprayed parchment paper on top of one half and roll it out as thin as possible. Aim for the thickness of two quarters stacked and 12" around. Repeat with the other half of the dough.

5 Place each crust on a pizza pan and top each with half of the sauce and the white cheddar and provolone. Push the sauce and cheese out to the edge.

6 Bake for 7 minutes, then remove the pizzas from the oven and swirl half of the ricotta cheese on each pizza.

7 Bake for another 2–3 minutes. Garnish with the breadcrumbs, cut into triangles, and enjoy!

Grilled

One of the most common questions I field is how to successfully grill pizza. And, for a while, I really hesitated to answer, because there is so much "feel" to it. The method used here combines flavor and ease for your best pizza making. The dough is slightly denser (meaning lower in hydration) than the typical dough, allowing it to hold up on the grates a bit better. The doughs also include wine or beer, which pair incredibly nicely with the grilled flavor and add some lightness (needed to cut the otherwise dense dough).

GRILLED PIZZA DOUGH WITH WINE OR BEER

**MAKES ONE 12" PIZZA, ONE 8"–10" SQUARE PIZZA,
OR THREE 6" "NAAN" BREADS**

Ingredients
- 2½ cups (338g) **bread flour**
- ½ cup (120mL) **warm water**
- 1 teaspoon (4g) **sugar**
- 2 teaspoons (6g) **instant yeast**
- ⅓ cup (80mL) **sauvignon blanc or beer (neutral lagers work best)**
- 1 teaspoon (6g) **salt**
- 2 tablespoons (28g) **olive oil**

1 In your stand mixer or large bowl, gently combine the water, sugar, yeast, and 1 cup of flour. Let stand for 3 minutes.

2 Following the rest period, pour in the wine and begin to mix using the hook attachment on low. Gently pour in the remaining flour, salt, and olive oil.

3 Mix for 5 minutes on medium-low speed. Once mixed, form into a ball and cover with a clean towel to rise for 4 hours, punching down the dough every hour.

Prosciutto, Romano, and Pinot Noir Grilled Pizza

We begin with this prosciutto, Romano, and pinot noir grilled pizza, which has netted me several awards, so you know it's legit. A classic flavor combination of prosciutto and dates adds a sweet and salty element to this pie. Also note the wine in the dough, which adds depth to the entire dish—the dough will slightly caramelize during the cooking, taking the flavor to new levels.

The secret here is the wine in the dough, which makes for a super crisp, lightly sweet crust.

Ingredients

- Grilled pizza dough with wine, see page 189
- 1 ounce Romano, shaved
- 4 dates, chopped
- 4 slices prosciutto ham
- 10 basil leaves, torn
- Olive oil, for drizzling

Equipment

- Gas or charcoal grill
- Pizza peel
- ⅓ cup vegetable oil (or any neutral oil)
- Tongs
- Paper towels

1 Prepare the dough.

2 Preheat your grill on high for 10 minutes. Gas or charcoal will work equally fine—the goal is 550°F (285°C). Remove any upper racks and ensure that the grates are spotless (any little bit will make your pizza stick).

3 As the grill heats, use a rolling pin to roll your dough into a 12" circle. Place the dough on a peel, making sure the dough can slide off easily. Be careful about using excess flour on your pizza, as it will burn quickly on the grill.

4 Lift the grill lid, dip a few paper towels in the vegetable oil, and use tongs to hold the paper towels and brush the oil onto the grates. There will be flames and hissing, and that's okay! Put the lid back down and let the flames subside for 2 minutes.

5 Cook the first side of the dough for 90 seconds with the lid closed, checking it often (the added wine can burn easily). Remove after the first cook and turn cooked side up onto the pizza peel.

6 Top the grilled side with the Romano, dates, and prosciutto.

7 Reoil the grates, then cook the pizza for 2–4 minutes (this is a longer cook since the grill will have cooled slightly). Check often for doneness—once the crust is set, the pizza is ready.

8 Once cooked, top with the basil and drizzle with olive oil. Cut and serve warm.

Garlic "Non-Naan"

Perhaps my favorite grilled pizza isn't actually pizza, but a play on the Indian flatbread known as naan. The sharp garlic and creamy butter are perfect counterpoints to the grilled char of the crust. This is a great side dish to standard grilled fare. Make them ahead of time on the hot clean grill, then store them wrapped in foil on the top rack of the grill as the remaining food cooks.

This isn't technically naan, but it's amazing just the same, and a go-to side when grilling pork or lamb.

Ingredients

- Grilled pizza dough with beer, see page 189
- 3 tablespoons butter, melted
- 4 cloves garlic, crushed
- ¼ cup chopped parsley

Equipment

- Gas or charcoal grill
- Pizza peel
- Paper towels
- ⅓ cup vegetable oil (or any neutral oil)
- Tongs

1 Prepare the dough.

2 Preheat your grill on high for 10 minutes. Gas or charcoal will work equally fine—the goal is 550°F (285°C). Remove any upper racks and ensure that the grates are spotless (any little bit will make your pizza stick).

3 As the grill heats, form your dough into three 6" rounds.

4 Lift the grill lid, dip a few paper towels in the vegetable oil, and use tongs to hold the paper towels and brush the oil onto the grates. There will be flames and hissing, and that's okay! Put the lid back down and let the flames subside for 2 minutes.

5 Cook the first side of the dough for 1–2 minutes, then open the lid and check on the underside. It should be a little dark, but not fully burnt. Depending on your grill, you should be able to cook all three at once. Sometime during cooking, brush the top of the dough with the butter and sprinkle on the garlic.

6 Flip the dough to cook the other side for 2–3 minutes. Remove and garnish with the parsley.

Grilled Margherita

Grilled pizza is one of the variants that is less about the region than it is about style or technique. That said, however, some of the best grilled pizza establishments are in the northeast. One of my favorites is Bar 'Cino, which has spots in both Rhode Island and Massachusetts. Derived from *vicino*, the Italian word for "neighbor," Bar 'Cino (pronounced "chee–no") is an informal neighborhood restaurant offering Italian-inspired dishes, creative cocktails, and a diverse wine program in a lively, stylish setting. They have certainly perfected the art of the grilled pizza, and my favorite pie is their take on the Margherita. My recipe is a tribute to their classic. Less is certainly more when it comes to grilling pizza, so the use of Romano and herbs creates a punch of flavor without weighing the pizza down. Also, while we call this a Margherita, you'll notice we have omitted the classic mozzarella, making this more of a mix between a Margherita and marinara pie.

Ingredients

- Grilled pizza dough with beer, see page 189
- ½ cup passata
- 1 ounce Pecorino Romano, grated
- 1 teaspoon dried oregano
- 1 Roma tomato, sliced thin
- 10 torn basil leaves
- Sliced green onions, optional
- Olive oil for drizzling

Equipment

- Gas or charcoal grill
- Pizza peel
- Paper towels
- Tongs
- ⅓ cup vegetable oil (or any neutral oil)

1 Prepare the dough.

2 Preheat your grill on high for 10 minutes. Gas or charcoal will work equally fine—the goal is 550°F (285°C). Remove any upper racks and ensure that the grates are spotless (any little bit will make your pizza stick).

3 As the grill heats, use a rolling pin to roll your dough into an 8"–10" square. Place the dough on a peel, making sure the dough can slide off easily. Be careful about using excess flour on your pizza, as it will burn quickly on the grill.

4 Stage your toppings nearby (these next few minutes will go quickly). Lift the grill lid, dip a few paper towels in the vegetable oil, and use tongs to hold the paper towels and brush the oil onto the grates. There will be flames and hissing, and that's okay! Put the lid back down and let the flames subside for 2 minutes.

5 Slide the dough onto the grates. Cook the first side of the dough for 60–90 seconds, then open the lid and check on the underside of the pizza. It should be a little dark, but not fully burnt. Remove the dough from the grill and place it cooked side up onto the pizza peel. Close the grill.

6 Top the grilled side with dollops of the passata, sprinkles of the Pecorino Romano, and the tomato slices.

7 Reoil the grates, then cook the pizza for 2–4 minutes (this is a longer cook since the grill will have cooled slightly). Check often for doneness—once the crust is set, the pizza is ready.

8 Once cooked, top with the dried oregano, sliced green onions, and basil, along with a pinch of salt and a drizzle of olive oil. Cut and serve warm.

The grill marks absolutely make this pie, creating not only an amazing visual but a charred flavor that is wonderful against the delicate toppings.

■ *Inspiration:*
This elegant pie from Bar 'Cino is a testament to "less is more." The green onions are more than garnish, as the sharp oniony bite plays with the grilled and sweet flavors nicely.

Caramelized Onion, Roasted Garlic, and Mushroom Grilled Pizza

Devised by my culinary team, this combination of caramelized onion, roasted garlic, and mushrooms is an utter masterclass in flavor and texture. The sweet and savory flavors from the alliums and mushrooms mesh wonderfully with the smoky, charred flavors of the dough. Finished with the tangy Romano, this pie is a total symphony of flavors!

A pizza adorned with classic French flavors, the long-cooked onion and garlic add their signature sweet and savory notes to make this slice akin to a good French onion soup.

Ingredients

- Grilled pizza dough with wine, see page 189
- ¼ cup roasted garlic (about 1 head's worth)
- 4 tablespoons olive oil, plus more for drizzling
- ½ cup caramelized onions
- 4 ounces button mushrooms, chopped and sautéed
- 2 ounces Romano, shaved
- 2 tablespoons chopped parsley

Equipment

- Gas or charcoal grill
- Pizza peel
- ⅓ cup vegetable oil (or any neutral oil)
- Tongs

1 Prepare the dough and combine the olive oil and garlic to create a loose paste.

2 Preheat your grill on high for 10 minutes. Gas or charcoal will work equally fine—the goal is 550°F (285°C). Remove any upper racks and ensure that the grates are spotless (any little bit will make your pizza stick).

3 Lift the grill lid, dip a few paper towels in the vegetable oil, and use tongs to hold the paper towels and brush the oil onto the grates. There will be flames and hissing, and that's okay! Put the lid back down and let the flames subside for 2 minutes.

4 As the grill heats, use a rolling pin to roll your dough into a 12" circle. Place the dough on a peel, making sure the dough can slide off easily. Be careful about using excess flour on your pizza, as it will burn quickly on the grill.

5 Cook the first side of the dough for 90 seconds, with the lid closed, checking it often. Remove after the first cook and turn cooked side up onto the pizza peel.

6 Brush the top of the dough with the garlic paste, then top with the onions, mushrooms, and Romano.

7 Reoil the grates, then cook the pizza for 2–4 minutes (this is a longer cook since the grill will have cooled slightly). Check often for doneness—once the crust is set, the pizza is ready.

8 Once cooked, top with the parsley and drizzle with olive oil. Cut and serve warm.

Trenton

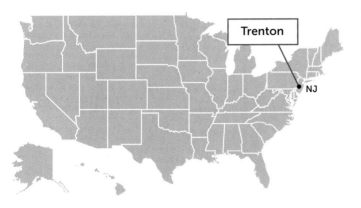

Trenton tomato pie, also known as New Jersey tomato pie, is a round, thin tomato pie created in Trenton, New Jersey, in the 1900s. This is a unique pie, as it is paper thin, with the cheese going down first and fusing with the dough—making almost a cracker for the toppings and sauce to sit upon. This dough is incredibly delicate, so if you have trouble, roll the dough out onto greased foil or parchment and place that on the pan.

TRENTON TOMATO PIE DOUGH

MAKES ONE 14" PIZZA

Ingredients
- **1½ cups (202g) bread flour**
- **½ cup (118mL) water**
- **1 teaspoon (5g) olive oil**
- **½ teaspoon (3g) salt**
- **2 teaspoons (6g) active dry yeast**

1 Add the water and oil to the work bowl of your stand mixer. With the hook attachment on low, slowly add in the flour, followed by the salt and yeast.

2 Work for 8 minutes, scraping down the sides every few minutes as needed.

3 Remove the dough from the bowl and form it into a ball. Place it back into the work bowl and let it set at room temperature for 1 hour.

4 Following the hour rise, move the dough to a large, nonstick spray–coated container. Cover the dough and refrigerate for 24–48 hours.

5 On pizza day, remove the dough from the fridge 2 hours before baking.

Trenton Tomato Pie with Cheese

When I think of a Trenton tomato pie, Classico Tomato Pies in West Windsor, New Jersey, immediately comes to mind. Here, they do it right, covering shredded mozzarella with squeezed whole tomatoes and olive oil to make one of the best-textured pies on the planet. This is one of those pies where the passion for the craft shows through, and pizza master Steve Cabrera is one of the finest, most passionate pizzaiolos in the area. Our version emulates the general style, with the cheese under the sauce and the use of canned whole tomatoes, which adds a wonderful texture to the pie.

Ingredients

- Trenton tomato pie dough, see page 195
- 6 ounces mozzarella, grated
- 1 cup canned whole tomatoes
- 1 tablespoon Italian seasoning
- 2 tablespoons olive oil for drizzling

Equipment

- 14" pizza pan
- Aluminum foil or pizza peel
- Nonstick spray

1 On pizza day, remove the dough from the fridge 2 hours before baking.

2 Preheat the oven to 475°F (245°C).

3 Once the dough is relaxed, roll it out into a 14" circle.

4 Top with the cheese first, then crush the tomatoes over the pie. Finish with the Italian seasoning. Push the sauce right out to the edge.

5 Bake on the pan 10–12 minutes until it's golden. Finish with a drizzle of olive oil and enjoy.

It's impossible not to love the caramelized bits of sauce on this, especially when paired with the fruitiness of the olive oil drizzle.

Inspiration:
This is tomato goodness from Classico—those dark spots are pure flavor, where the tomatoes have been kissed by the oven to create savory, textural hot spots.

Marinara Trenton Pie

This pie, admittedly, is not entirely typical, but I landed upon it while recipe testing and thought it was wildly delicious. The base is the Trenton tomato pie dough, but the pie is topped like a Neapolitan marinara (no cheese, just sauce and garlic). The result is a really wonderful slice—clean, crisp, and tomato-forward.

Ingredients

- Trenton tomato pie dough, see page 195
- 1 cup canned whole tomatoes
- 3 cloves garlic, sliced thin
- 1 teaspoon dried oregano
- 2 tablespoons extra-virgin olive oil for drizzling

Equipment

- 14" pizza pan
- Aluminum foil or pizza peel
- Nonstick spray

1 On pizza day, remove the dough from the fridge two hours before baking.

2 Preheat the oven to 475°F (245°C).

3 Once the dough is relaxed, roll it out into a 14" circle.

4 Crush the tomatoes over the pie, sprinkle on the garlic, and finish with the oregano. Push the sauce right out to the edge.

5 Bake on the pan 10–12 minutes until it's golden. Finish with a drizzle of olive oil.

This is a wonderful pie invented as a byproduct of recipe testing. Here the tomato flavors shine, kissed by the heat of the oven.

Quad Cities

Quad Cities-style pizza (hailing from the Quad Cities region in Western Illinois and Eastern Iowa) is truly one of the more interesting and slept-on pizzas in this book. The crust is thin like a Chicago tavern style, but interestingly sweet and spicy due to the addition of malt syrup and cayenne pepper. The pizza is cut into strips, and sweet fennel sausage is a mainstay. The result is a pizza that is sweet, spicy, and one of the more complex pies you will ever enjoy. The dough is a lower-hydration dough, though the malt syrup helps it come together. As a result, more patience is needed when rolling out, so plan accordingly.

Quad Cities

QUAD CITIES DOUGH

MAKES ONE 14" PIZZA

Ingredients
- 2 cups (270g) **bread flour**
- ½ cup plus a splash (130mL) **bottled water**
- 1 tablespoon (22g) **malt syrup**
- ½ teaspoon (3g) **salt**
- ½ teaspoon (1.5g) **active dry yeast**
- ½ teaspoon (1g) **cayenne pepper**

1 In your stand mixer using the hook attachment or a large bowl using your hands, combine all the dough ingredients.

2 Mix for 10 minutes, then roll the dough into a ball and let it rise on the counter for 30 minutes.

3 After the rise, refrigerate the dough overnight for up to 3 days.

4 Remove the dough from the refrigerator 4 hours before cooking and let it come to room temperature.

QUAD CITIES SAUCE

MAKES ONE 14" PIZZA

Ingredients
- 2 tablespoons **olive oil**
- 1 tablespoon **minced garlic**
- ½ cup **crushed tomatoes**
- 1 teaspoon **oregano**
- 1 teaspoon **black pepper**
- ½ teaspoon **red pepper flakes**
- ½ teaspoon **salt**

1 Add the oil and garlic to a saucepot over low heat and sweat for 2 minutes.

2 Add the tomatoes, oregano, black pepper, red pepper, and salt. Raise the heat to a simmer and cook for 10 minutes.

3 Keep cool until ready to cook.

Quad Cities Cheese Pizza

One of the original and classic Quad Cities spots is Harris Pizza, with several locations in the greater Quad Cities area. Founded by Len and Mary Harris in 1960, Harris Pizza embodies everything great about this style of pie. In fact, they own the trademark to the phrase "Finest Pizza in the World," which I can't dispute! This version certainly mirrors the malty, spicy elements in the dough—signature flavors of the regional style. Don't be surprised if this dough is a bit more challenging than some others—given the hydration levels and malt syrup, it can be a tad fussy. If the dough really fights you, let it relax for 5–10 minutes before shaping again.

The corner piece, where the cheese gets extra melty and the crust is perfectly cooked, is the absolute best piece.

■ **Inspiration:**
I love how deeply rich the crust is on a Harris Pizza creation because of the molasses and cayenne notes.

Ingredients
- Quad Cities dough, see page 200
- Quad Cities sauce, see page 200
- 8 ounces mozzarella cheese, grated
- 1 teaspoon dried oregano

Equipment
- 14" pizza pan
- Kitchen shears, optional

1 Sometime before pizza day, prepare the dough and sauce.

2 Remove the dough from the refrigerator 4 hours before cooking and let it come to room temperature.

3 Preheat the oven to 450°F (230°C).

4 Stretch the dough into a 12"–14" circle with a slight lip. Transfer to the pan.

5 Thinly sauce the pizza, then finish with the cheese and oregano.

6 Bake for 12–16 minutes or until very bubbly and brown. Let cool and, if you want to be authentic, cut it into strips with kitchen shears to enjoy.

Quad Cities Sausage Pizza

It's hard to imagine a Quad Cities pizza without its signature sweet fennel sausage. The way the spicy fennel plays with and against the malt syrup and cayenne in the dough is utterly magnificent. Harris Pizza, unsurprisingly, has some of the finest (and tangiest) sausage in the area, which is probably why I love it so much. Our take is similar to the classic Quad Cities pie, though I personally enjoy the texture of larger sausage crumbles. The choice is yours!

Ingredients

- Quad Cities dough, see page 200
- Quad Cities sauce, see page 200
- 1 teaspoon fennel seed, divided
- ½ pound sweet Italian sausage, bulk
- 10 ounces mozzarella cheese, grated
- 1 teaspoon dried oregano

Equipment

- 14" pizza pan
- Kitchen shears, optional

1 Sometime before pizza day, prepare the dough and prepare the sauce, adding ½ teaspoon of the fennel seed with the oil and garlic in sauce step 1.

2 Also before pizza day, heat a frying pan over medium heat. Add the bulk sausage and cook for 2–3 minutes, then begin to break it up into small crumbles with a spatula or wooden spoon. Continue cooking the sausage for 8–10 minutes, stirring frequently until it is evenly browned and has reached an internal temperature of 165°F (74°C).

3 Remove the dough from the refrigerator 4 hours before cooking and let it come to room temperature.

4 Preheat the oven to 450°F (230°C).

5 Stretch the dough into a 12"–14" circle with a slight lip. Transfer to the pan.

6 Thinly sauce the pizza, then top with the remaining fennel seed, prepared sausage, cheese, and oregano.

7 Bake for 13–17 minutes or until very bubbly and brown. Let cool and, if you want to be authentic, cut it into strips with kitchen shears to enjoy.

For a changeup, try chorizo on this pizza in place of the sausage—the warm spices in the meat will play with the sauce and crust perfectly.

■ *Inspiration:* All of the wonderful fennel sausage against the complex crust creates a very unusual but sweet and savory bite that is unique to Harris Pizza's pie.

Quad Cities Taco Pizza

Taco pizza is a delightful fusion of two beloved cuisines, combining the savory flavors of a taco with the cheesy goodness of pizza. The spicy Quad Cities–style crust provides a robust foundation that enhances seasoned ground beef and taco spices. The heat from the crust contrasts beautifully against cool toppings like lettuce and tomatoes, creating a balanced taste profile. Finally, the cheese adds a creamy richness, melding all the flavors together seamlessly. This pie is more than a gimmick or forced mashup—it's a perfect example of what Quad Cities pizza can do.

The texture from the chips and lettuce is perfect against the crisp crust and melty cheese.

Ingredients

- Quad Cities dough, see page 200
- Quad Cities sauce, see page 200
- ¼ teaspoon fennel seed
- 8 ounces ground beef
- 3 tablespoons taco seasoning
- 1 cup mozzarella, grated
- 1 cup cheddar, grated
- 1 cup shredded lettuce
- 1 cup diced tomato
- 1 cup crushed corn chips

Equipment

- 14" pizza pan

1 Sometime before pizza day, prepare the dough and prepare the sauce, adding the fennel seed with the oil and garlic in sauce step 1.

2 Also before pizza day, heat a frying pan over medium heat. Add the ground beef and cook for 2–3 minutes, then begin to break it up into small crumbles with a spatula or wooden spoon. Continue cooking the ground beef for 6–8 minutes, stirring frequently until it is evenly browned and has reached an internal temperature of 165°F (74°C). Add the taco seasoning and cook for another 2–3 minutes, then keep cool until ready to use.

3 Preheat the oven to 450°F (230°C). Remove the dough from the fridge.

4 Stretch the dough into a 12"–14" circle with a slight lip. Transfer to the pan.

5 Thinly sauce the pizza, then top with the prepared ground beef and the cheeses.

6 Bake for 13–17 minutes or until very bubbly and brown. Let cool and cut into traditional pizza slices.

7 Top with the lettuce, tomato, and corn chips and serve.

New Jersey Boardwalk

New Jersey boardwalk pizza is tied to the region more than just about any other style. Best enjoyed on the beach at an open-air restaurant, this pie is a staple when cruising the pier. This pizza is a perfect dichotomy of textured and bready, sweet and salty, familiar yet interesting. The signature sauce swirl on top is the perfect finish for a pizza that is delightfully crisp.

NEW JERSEY BOARDWALK DOUGH

MAKES ONE 14" PIZZA

Ingredients
- **2 cups** (270g) **bread flour**
- **⅔ cup** (158mL) **water**
- **1 teaspoon** (3g) **active dry yeast**
- **1½ teaspoons** (6g) **sugar**
- **1 teaspoon** (6g) **salt**
- **1 tablespoon** (13g) **shortening**

1 In your stand mixer or a large bowl, gently combine the water, yeast, sugar, and 1 cup of the flour. Let stand for 10 minutes.

2 Following the rest period, begin to mix using the hook attachment on your stand mixer on low. Gently pour in the remaining flour, salt, and shortening.

3 Mix for 5 minutes on medium-low speed (scraping the bowl as needed to keep the dough in the bowl).

4 Once mixed, form the dough into a ball and cover it with plastic wrap. Let it rise on the counter for 2 hours, then punch it down, re-form it into a ball, and keep it in the fridge for 1–2 days.

5 Remove the dough from the fridge 2 hours before cooking.

New Jersey Boardwalk Pizza

My all-time favorite boardwalk pie is from Maruca's Tomato Pies, which has locations in Seaside Heights and Asbury Park, both in New Jersey. Here they make (and made famous) amazing boardwalk pies and have been doing so since 1950. Maruca's also features a signature sauce swirl, which is as visually appealing as it gets. Trust me when I say that the team at Maruca's is as passionate and as skilled as they come—it was certainly a pleasure talking to Dominic Maruca about pizza, the business, and everything in between! Our version of this boardwalk classic borrows inspiration, with the signature swirl and light and crisp crust. Their pies also go up to 24"—probably a bit large for in-home ovens, so we will scale things back. While their specific dough, cheese blends, and sauce recipes are their secret, this recipe will certainly remind you of a warm summer day in New Jersey!

Ingredients

- New Jersey boardwalk dough, see page 205
- 1 cup crushed tomatoes
- 1 tablespoon dried oregano
- 1 teaspoon garlic salt
- ¼ teaspoon ground black pepper
- 7 ounces white cheddar, grated

Equipment

- 14" pizza pan
- Small pitcher or similar tool, for swirling sauce

1 Sometime before pizza day, combine the crushed tomatoes, dried oregano, garlic salt, and black pepper. No cooking needed. Keep cool until ready to cook.

2 Remove the dough from the fridge 2 hours before cooking.

3 Preheat the oven to 475°F (245°C).

4 Place the dough ball on a floured surface and form it into a 14" circle, making a very subtle crust lip. Transfer it to the pan.

5 Top the pizza with the white cheddar and swirl on the sauce (I used a small pitcher with great results).

6 Bake for 10–14 minutes or until golden. Slice into massive pieces and enjoy!

The sauce swirl is more than a decoration, it also partially protects the cheese, making for waves of varying textures in each slice.

■ *Inspiration:* Maruca's pizzas always include that signature swirl you'll find on the boardwalk!

New Jersey White Boardwalk Pizza

Another boardwalk favorite is the white pie, a sauceless symphony of cheeses and textures. Here we will use ricotta, white cheddar, and Romano as our toppings, letting each flavor shine unchecked. If there is a secret to this white pie, it is the use of the highest-quality, lowest-moisture ricotta cheese you can find—a watery cheese will create a less-than-ideal texture on the pie!

Ingredients

- New Jersey boardwalk dough, see page 205
- 1 cup ricotta cheese
- 4 ounces white cheddar, grated
- 3 tablespoons Romano cheese, grated

Equipment

- 14" pizza pan

1 Remove the dough from the fridge 2 hours before cooking.

2 Preheat the oven to 475°F (245°C).

3 Place the dough ball on a floured surface and form it into a 14" circle, making a very subtle crust lip. Transfer it to the pan.

4 Top the pizza with the white cheddar, then add dollops of ricotta, and finally cover the pizza with the Romano.

5 Bake for 10–14 minutes or until golden. Slice into massive pieces and enjoy!

I love how the ricotta melts into the pie, making an ultra-creamy pizza that holds up due to the makeup of the dough.

Inspiration:
The range of cheeses in Maruca's creation makes for a very interesting slice that's surprisingly complex given the few ingredients used.

Index

Acknowledgments

This book featured many, many incredible pizza makers across the country. I would be remiss if I didn't use a bit of space to personally thank them and to tell you where you can find more from these incredible artists.

A special thank-you to my photography and culinary team, Joe Delnero (see @joe_delnero for more of his photography), Susan Murphy, Alice Murphy, Judy Murphy, and Gloria Mumford, who helped produce a truly epic pizza party and many of the pictures in this book.

Thank you to Christy Alia (@realcleverfood) and Jimmy Henry (@jimmyhank_pizza) for not only lending some shots for this book, but also being my pizza sounding board throughout this journey.

To Michael Fox (@ineedpizzaclub) and Will Dumas (@funniewill), my podcast producer and co-host, thank you for introducing me to many of the pizza masters within this book and for giving me a platform to discuss and debate regional styles of pizza every week.

Thank you to all of the pizza makers and restaurants mentioned in this book; you all provided the inspiration for the recipes here and I am grateful for the many years and millions of pizzas you have served to the world. Follow them here:

- Pepe's Pizzeria: @frankpepepizza
- Mercurio's: @mercuriospgh
- Dimo's: @dimospizza
- Sanctuary Pizza: @sanctuary_pizza
- Bar 'Cino: barcino.com
- TAGLIO: @tagliopizza
- Pa' Comer Cuban Pizza: @pizza_cubana
- Tiny Pizza Kitchen: @tinypizzakitchen
- Burt's Place: @burtsplacepizza
- The Art of Pizza: @theartofpizza_inc
- Pie Sci: @piescipizza
- Lancaster House of Pizza: lancasterhouseofpizza.com
- Beau Jo's Pizza: @beaujospizza
- Enzo's Pizza: @enzospizzabycrazypour
- Ohio Valley Pizza Company: @ohiovalleypizzacompany
- Pizza Fenice: @pizzafenice

- Squares & Fare: @squaresandfare
- Gaeta's Tomato Pies: @gaetastomatopie
- Avalon Downtown Pizzeria @avalondowntown
- La Casa Legendary Pizza & Pasta: lacasapizzaria.net
- Revello's Pizza: revellos.com
- Carbone's: @carbones716
- Geraci's Slice Shop: @geracissliceshop
- Flo & Santos: @floandsantos
- Monte Bello Pizzeria: montebellostl.wordpress.com
- Classico Tomato Pies: @classico.tomato.pies
- Harris Pizza: @harrispizza
- Don Antonio Pizza & Cocktails: @donantonionewyork
- Maruca's Tomato Pies: @marucaspizza
- John Carruthers: @nachosandlager

About the Author

Jim Mumford is a World Food Championships certified judge and a food writer whose recipes have featured at *MarthaStewart.com*, *Yahoo*, *NBC News*, *Reader's Digest*, *Huffington Post*, and more. As weekly co-host of a live pizza roundtable and specializing in pizza topics for *InsideHook*, he knows all things in the world of crust, sauce, and toppings. In covering 30 regional pizza styles across over 100 recipes, Mumford has created the best pizza cookbook for everyone from home cooks to die-hard pizza nerds in search of a comprehensive addition to their library. In *PizzaPedia*, he covers everything from classics like Chicago deep dish and Detroit-style to lesser-known regional pizzas like Ohio Valley and Old Forge.

Jim and his wife at Flo & Santos in Chicago years ago while they were still dating. Though they've since moved out of the area, they still make sure to come back often to their original date-night spot.

Author Jim Mumford making pizza in his home.

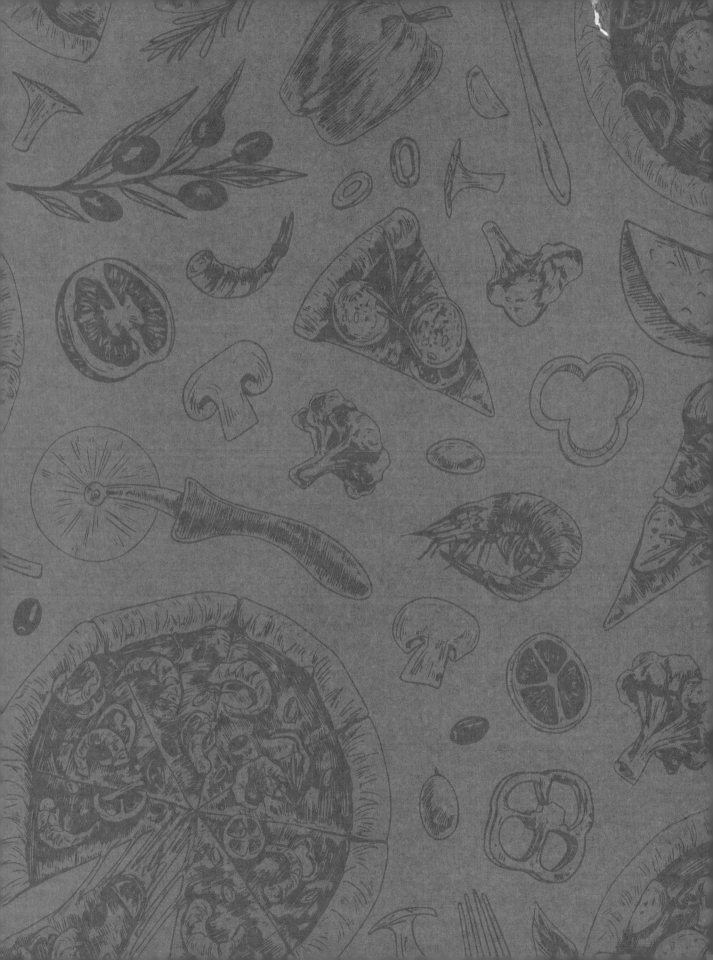